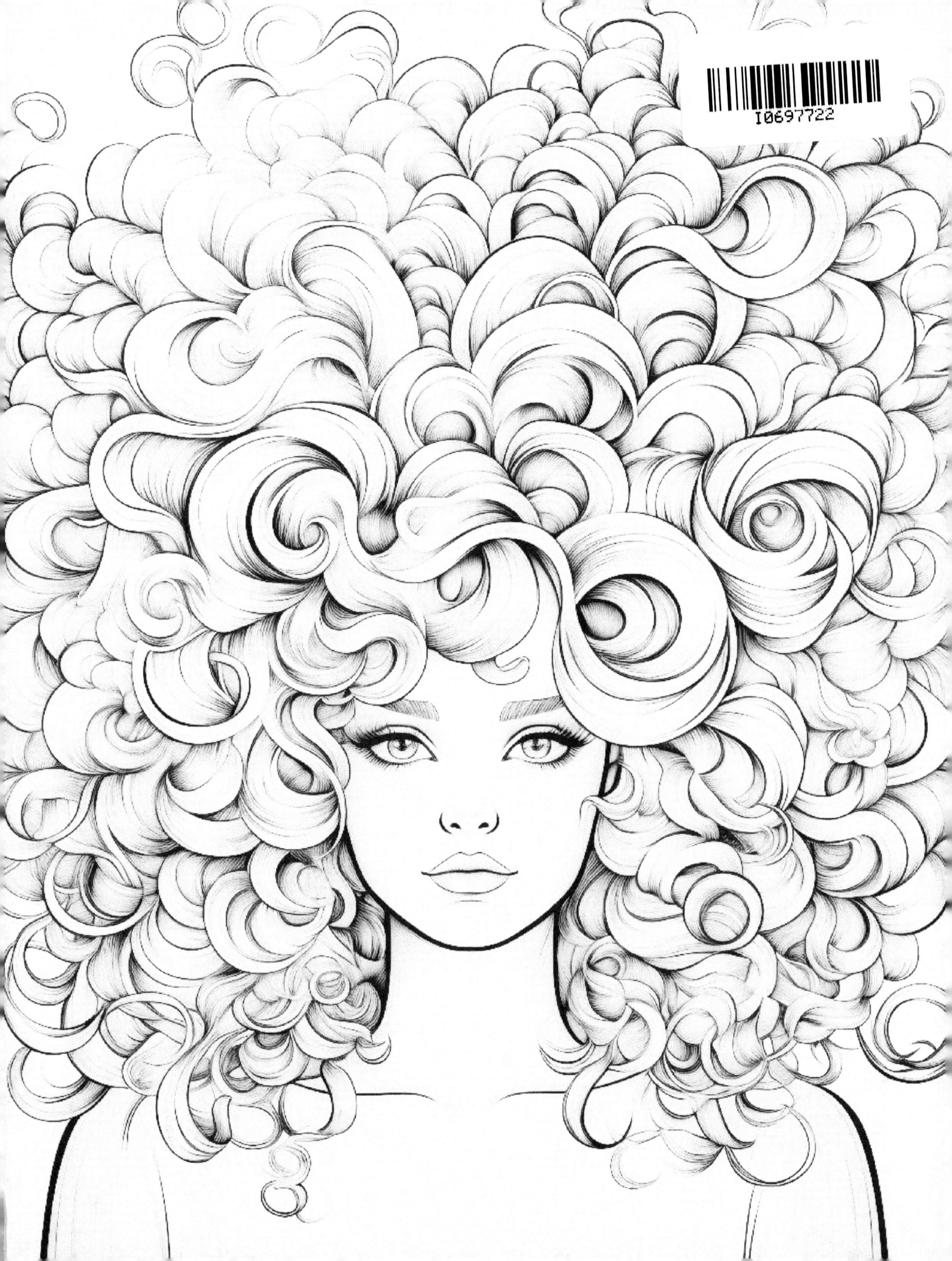

I0697722

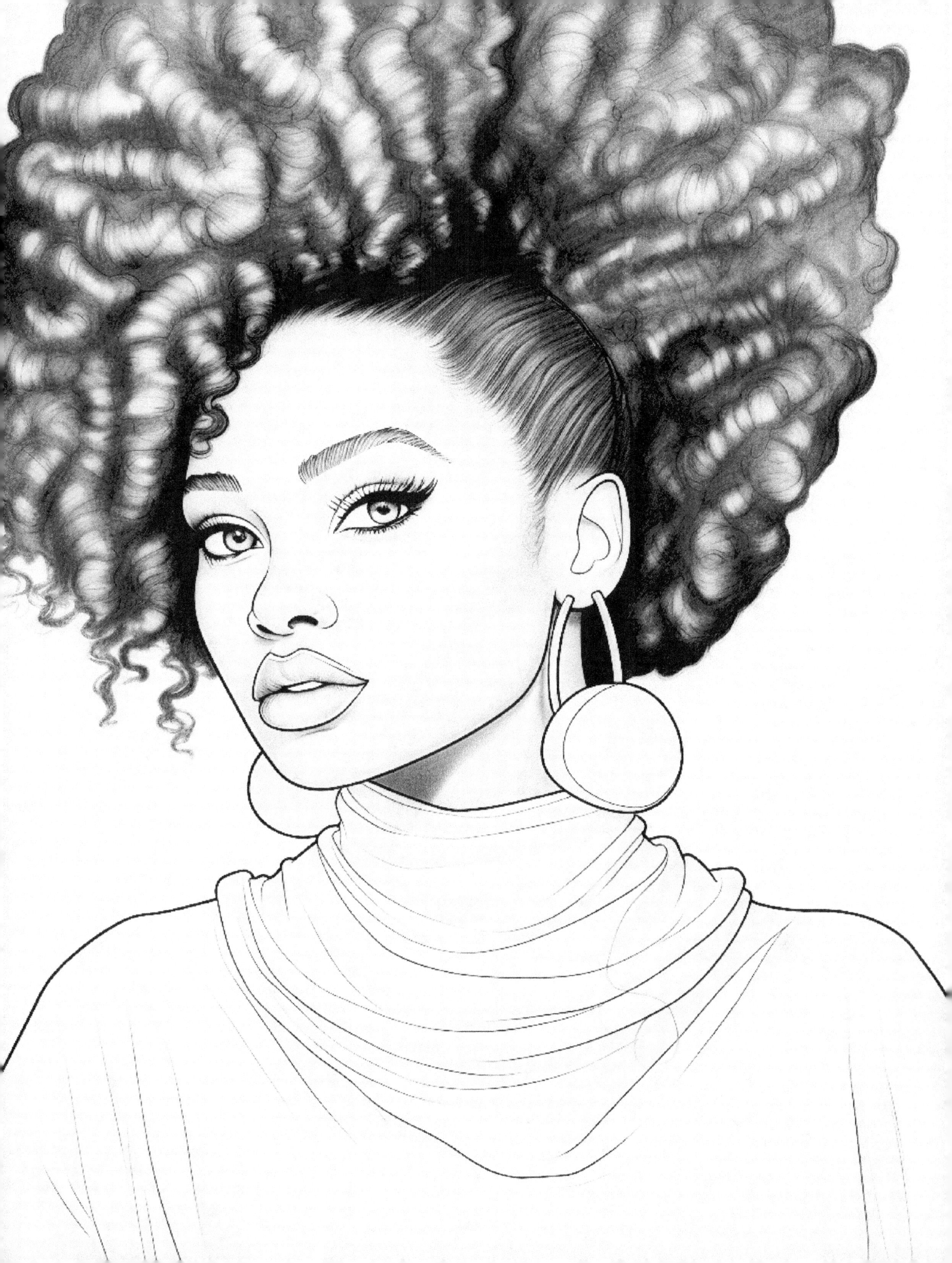

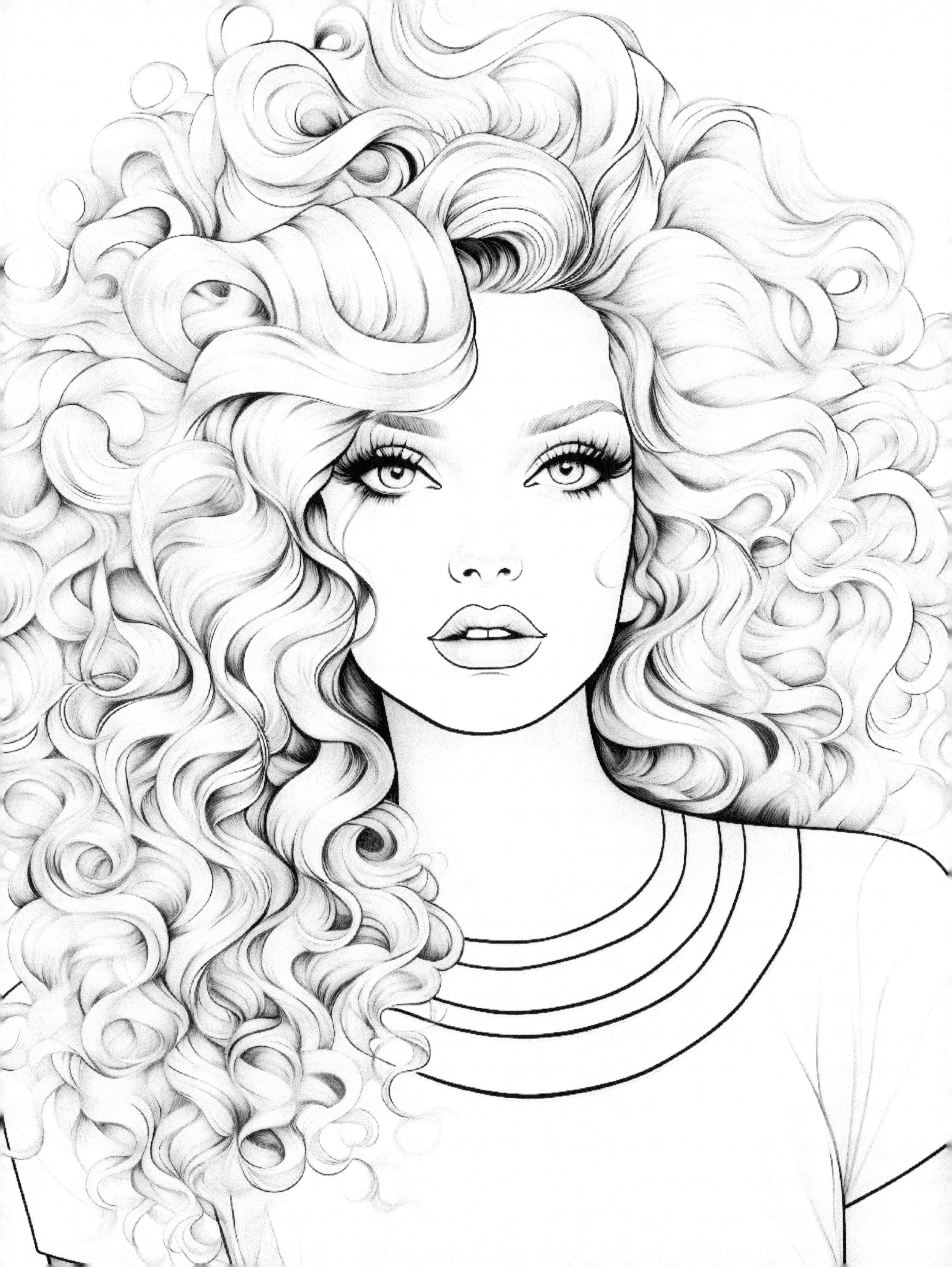

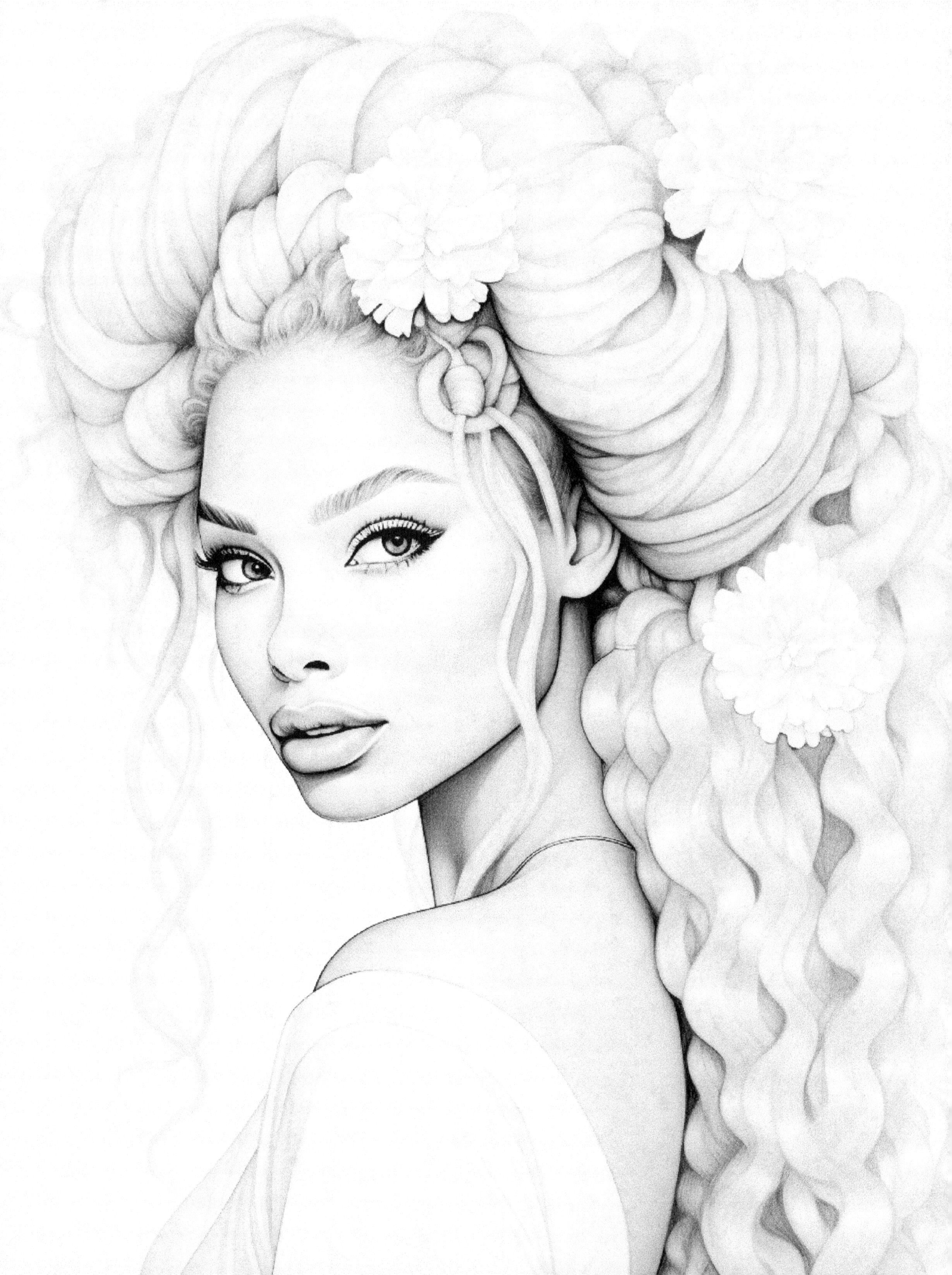

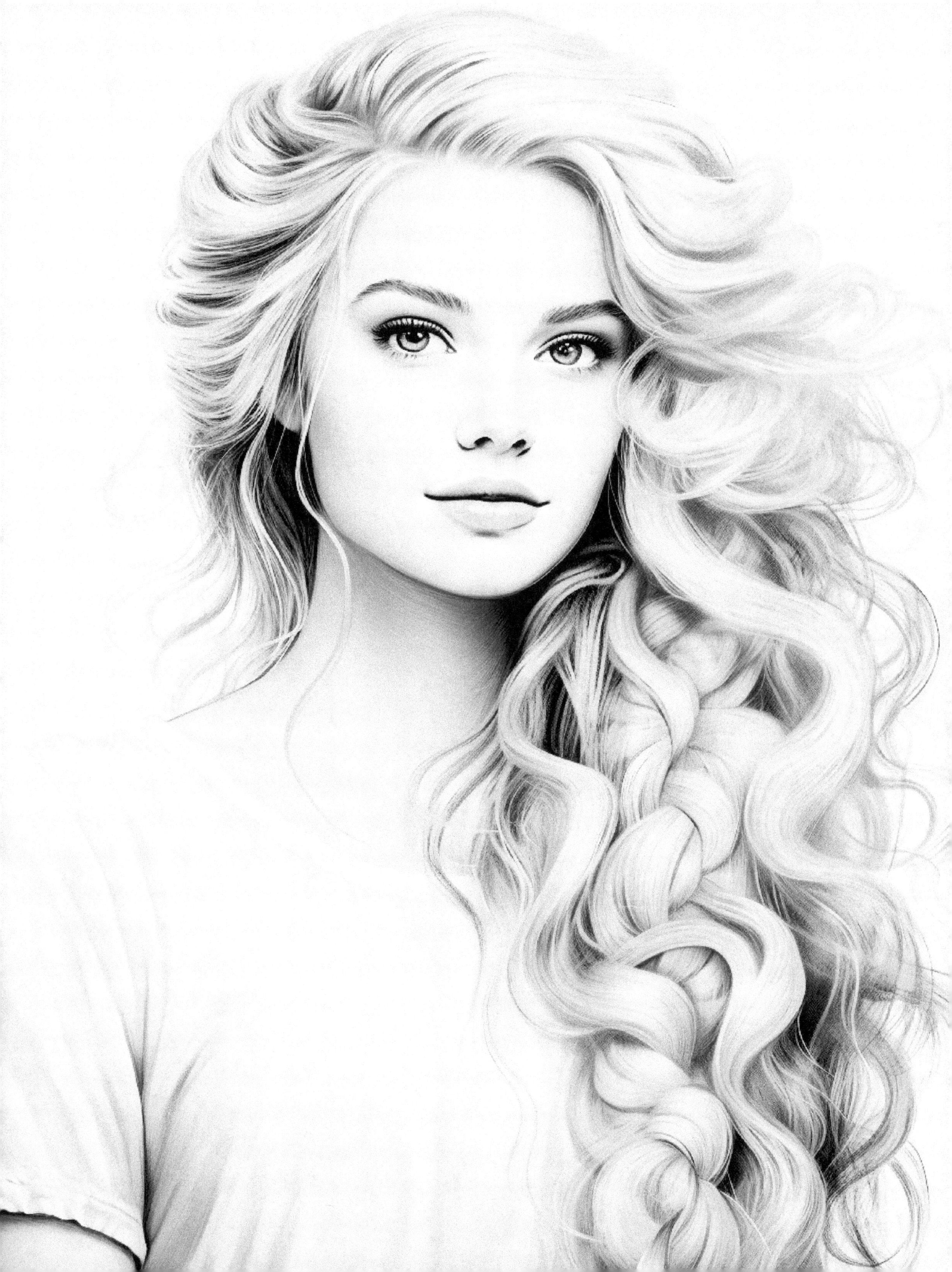

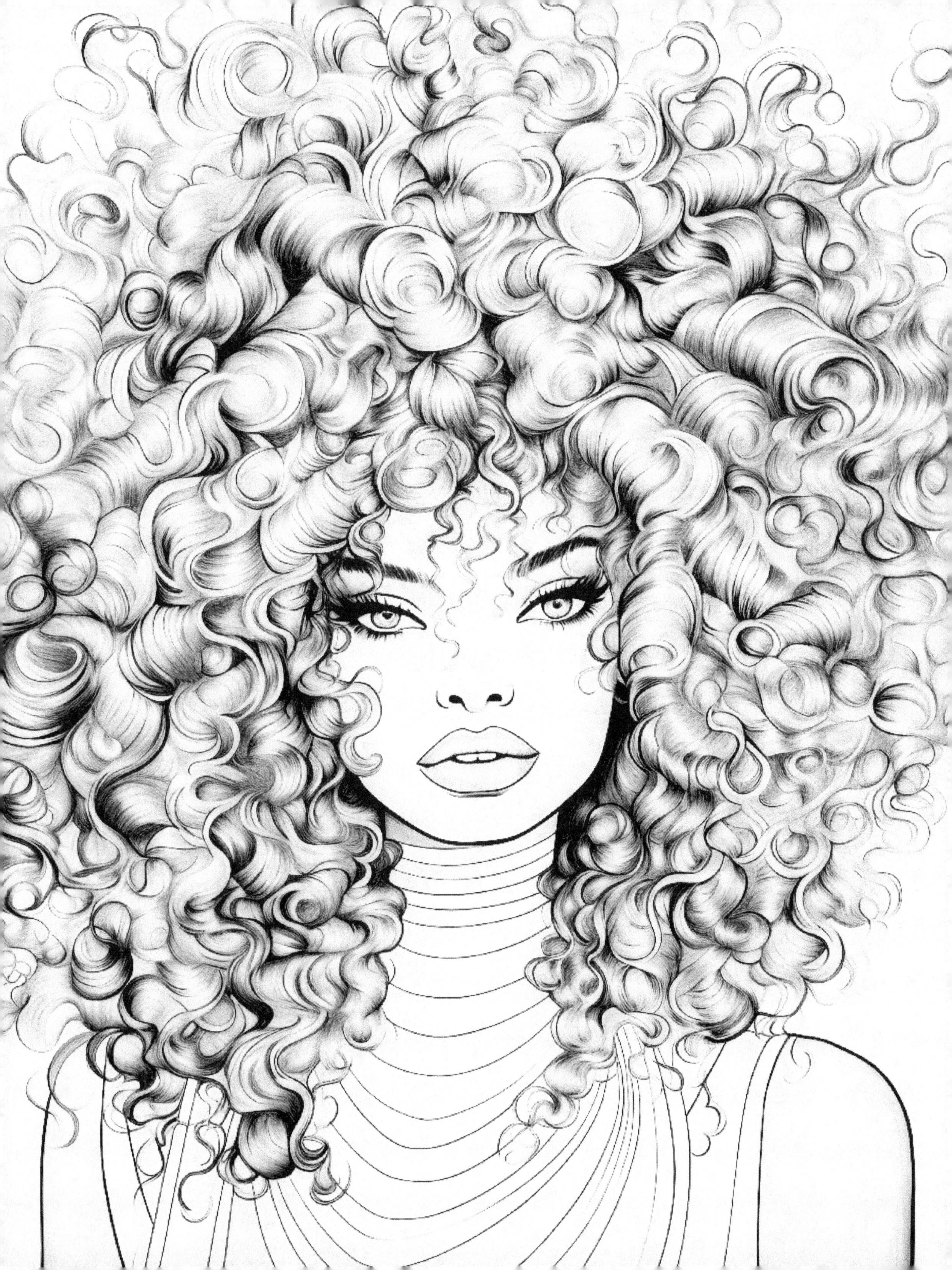

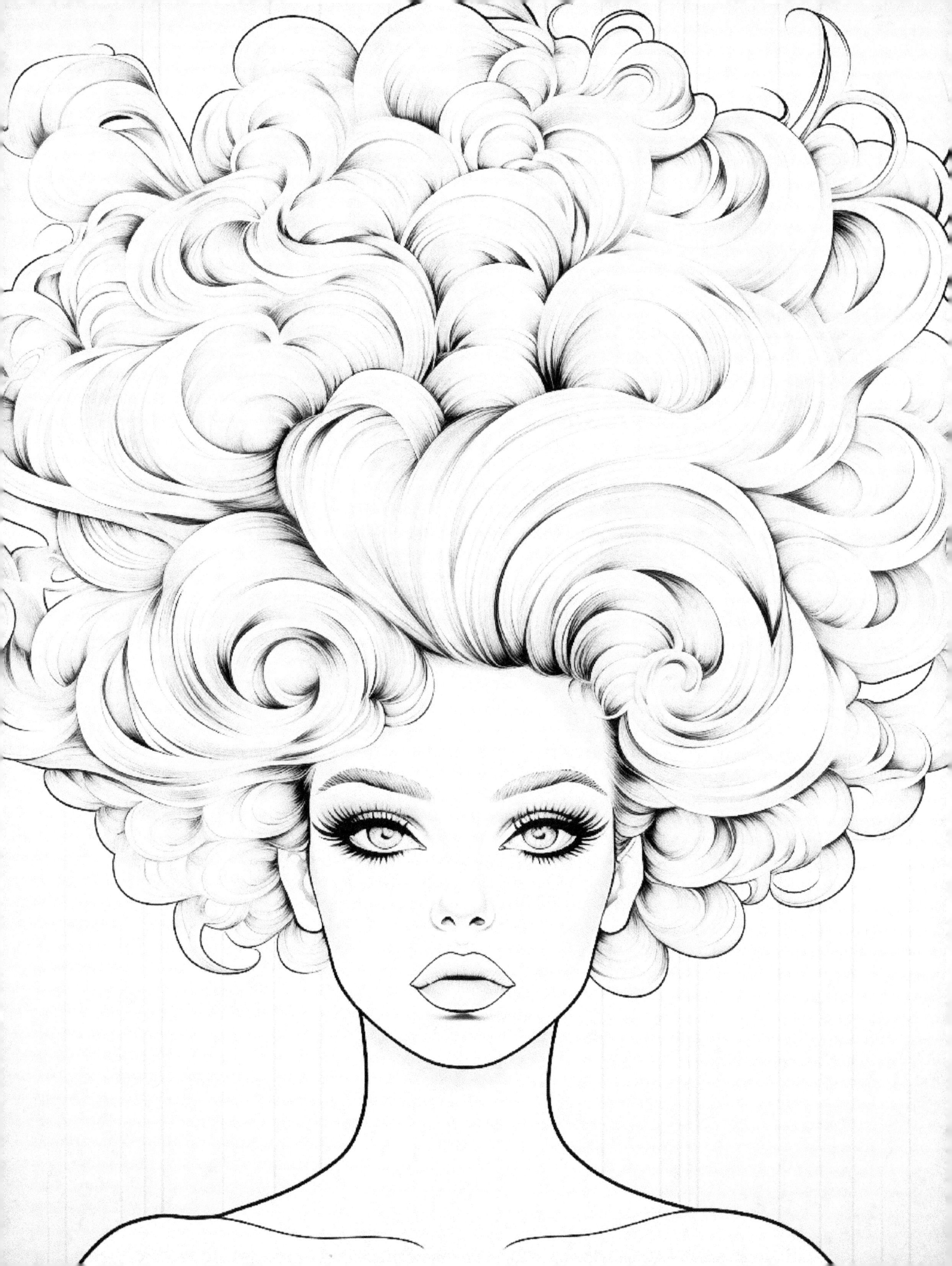

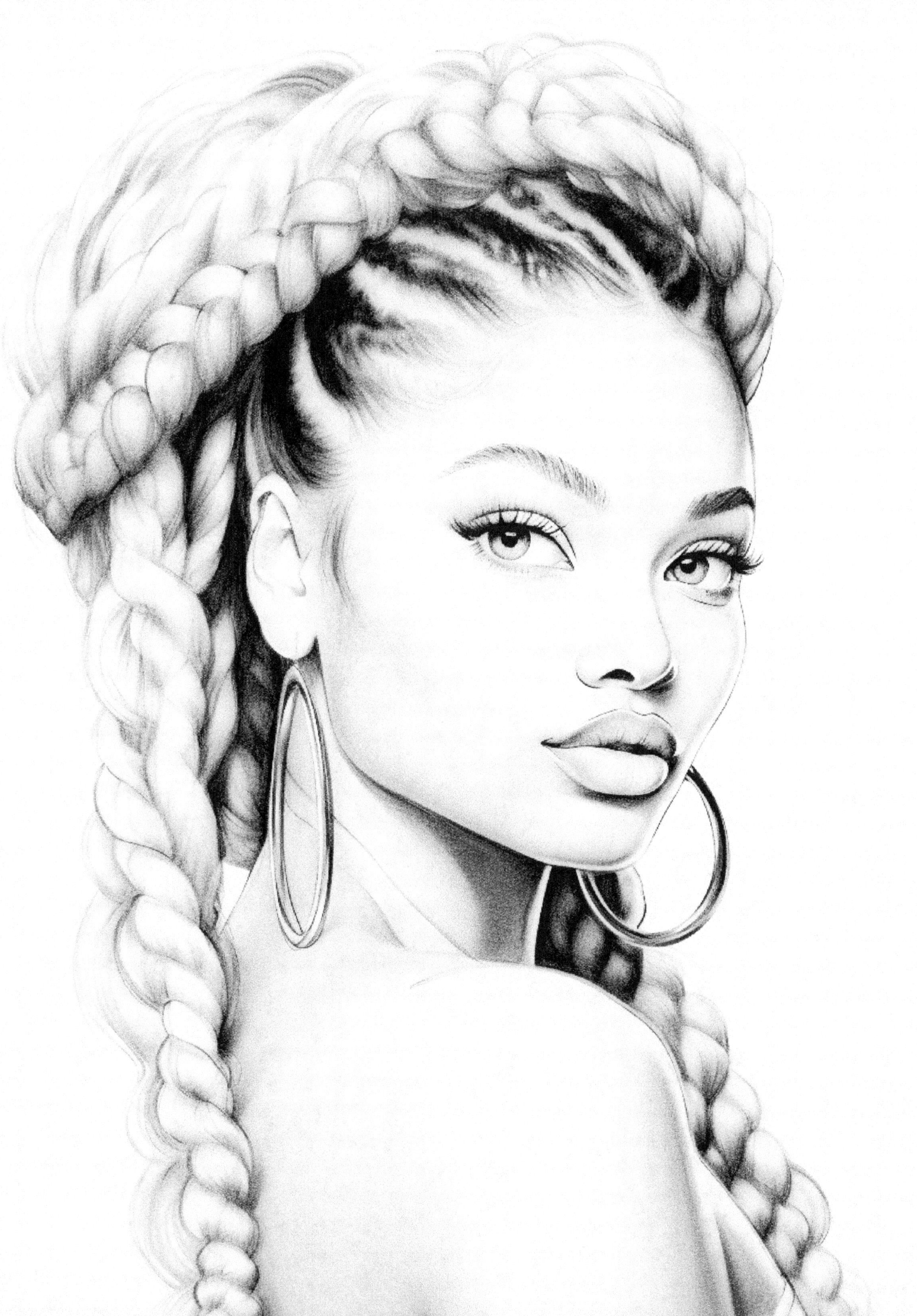

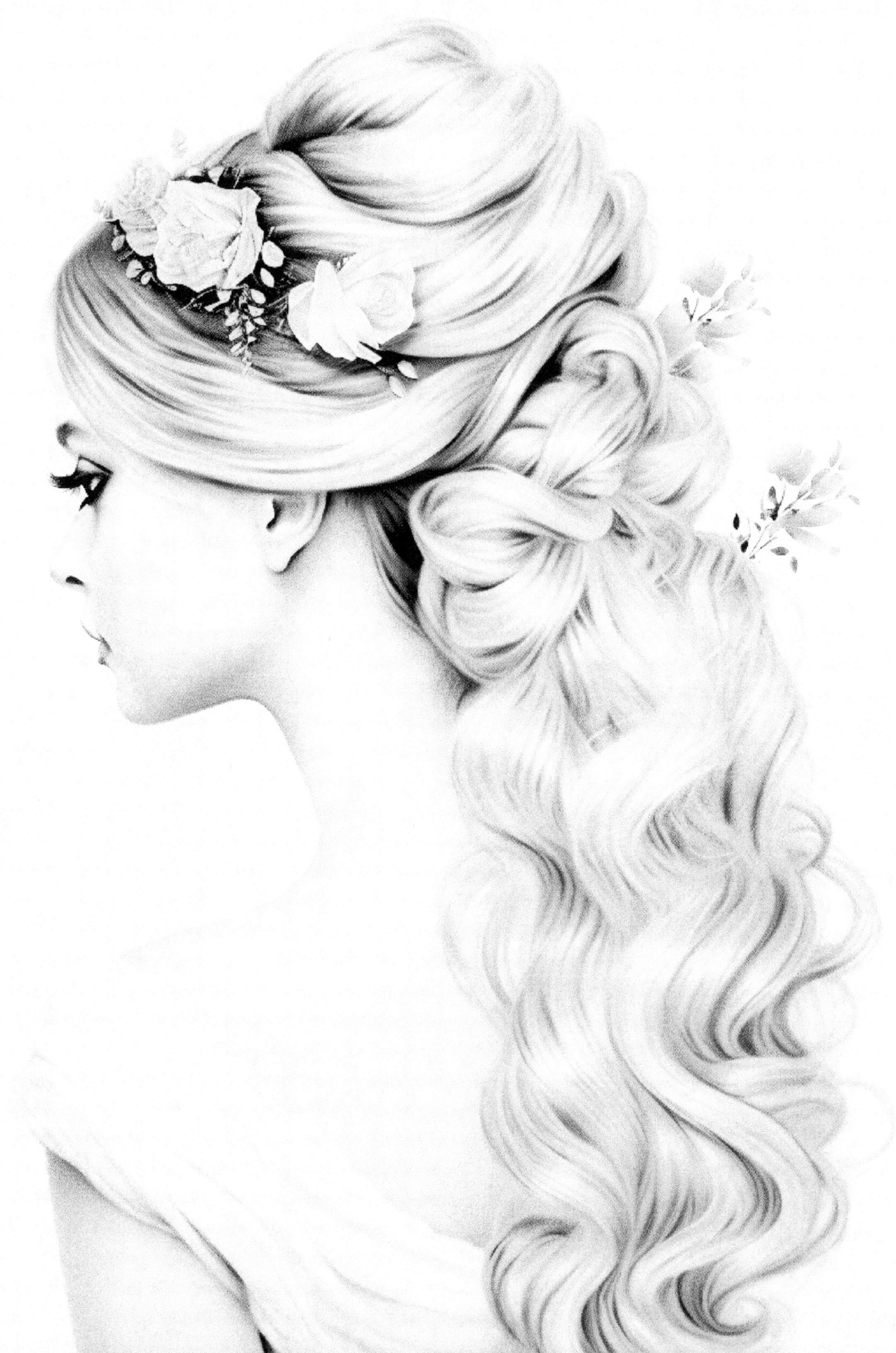

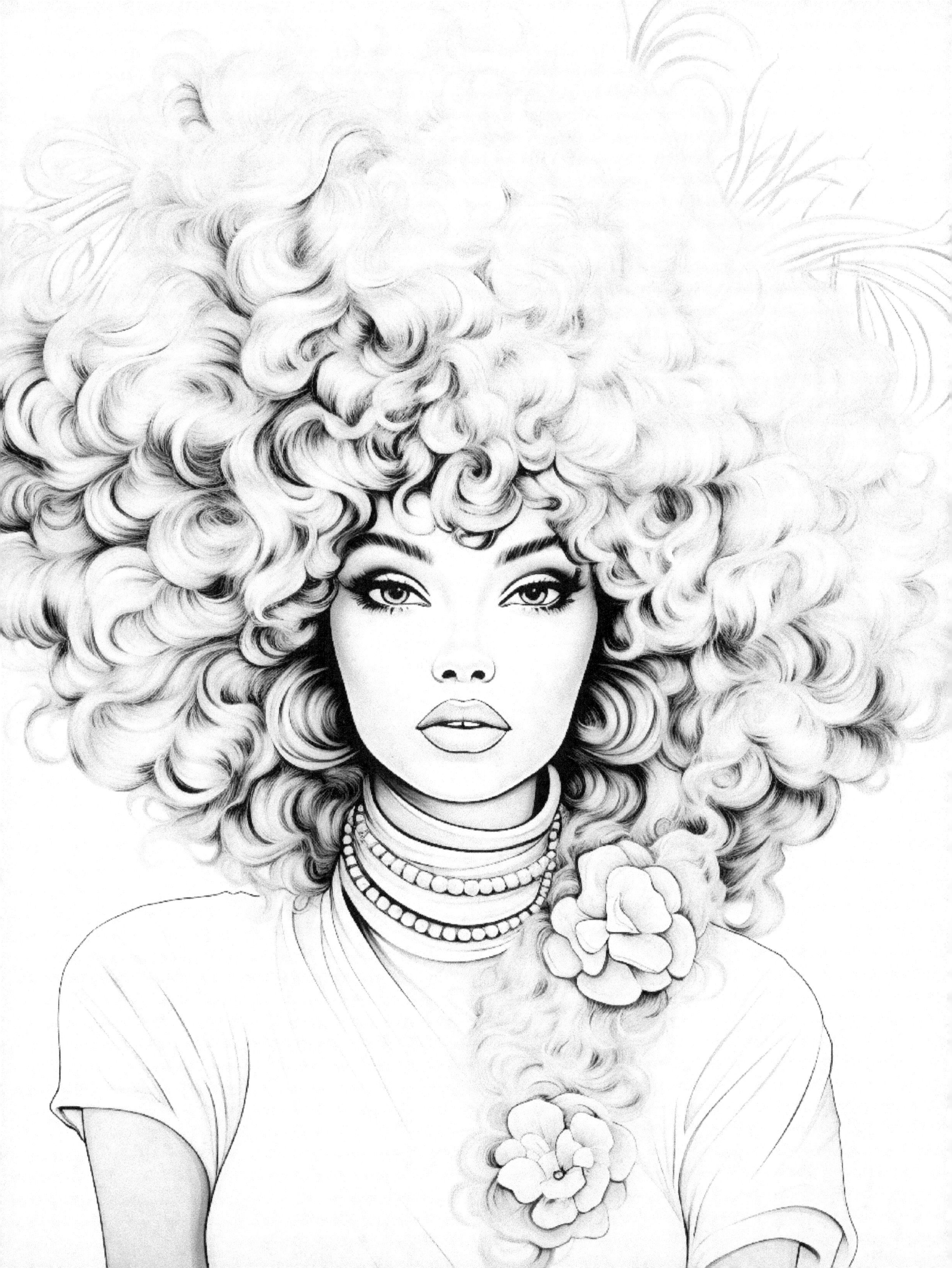

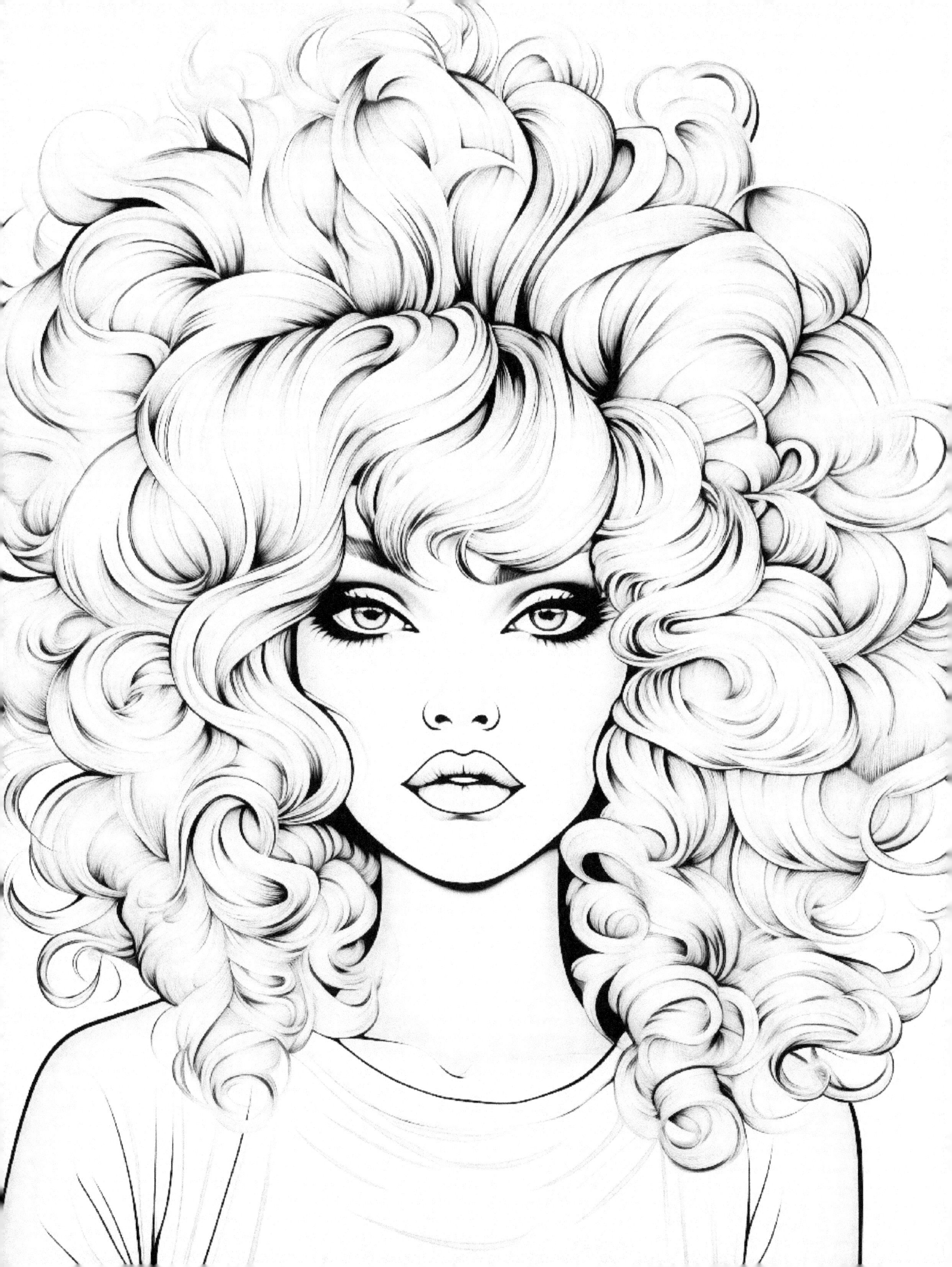

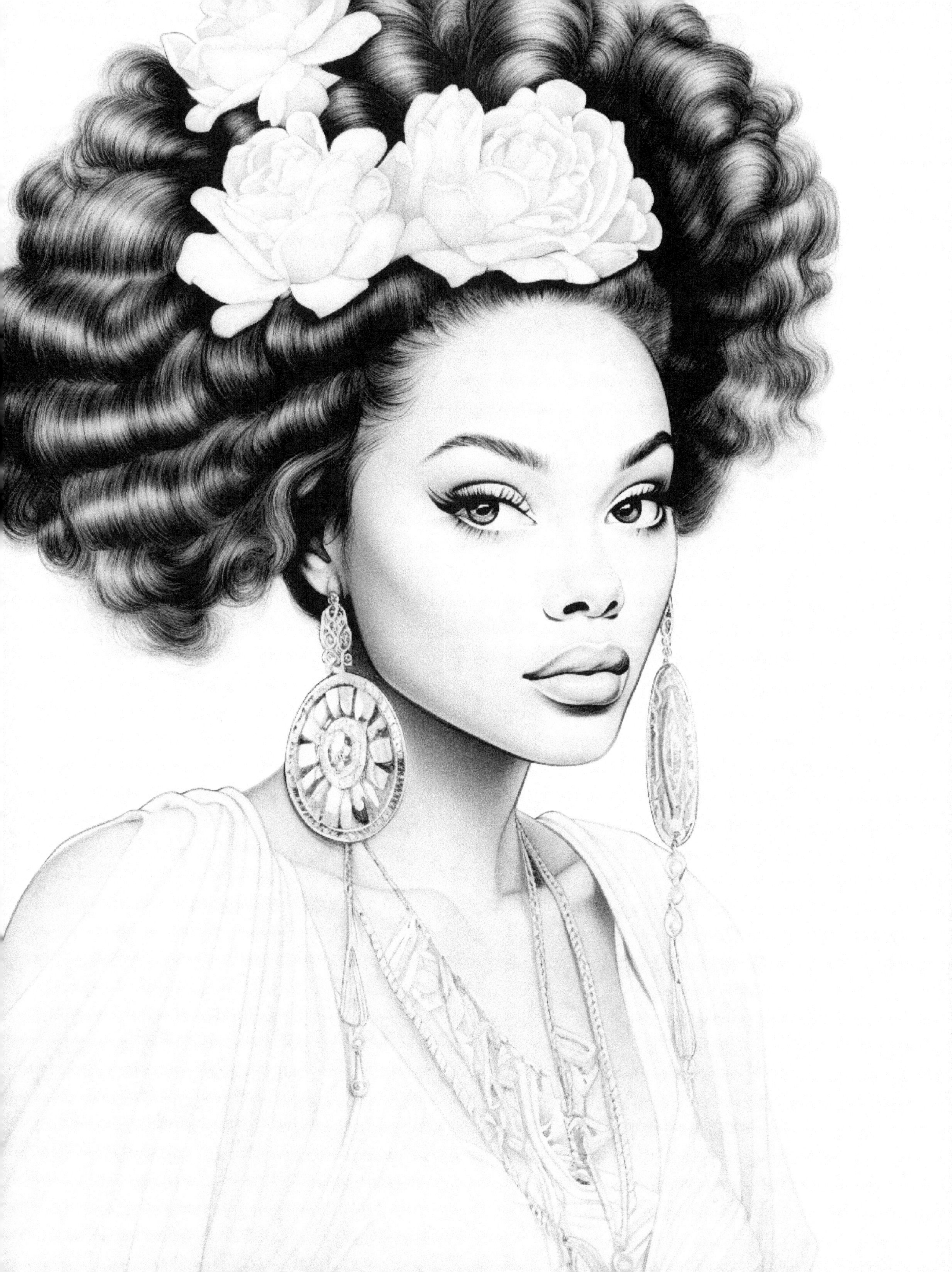

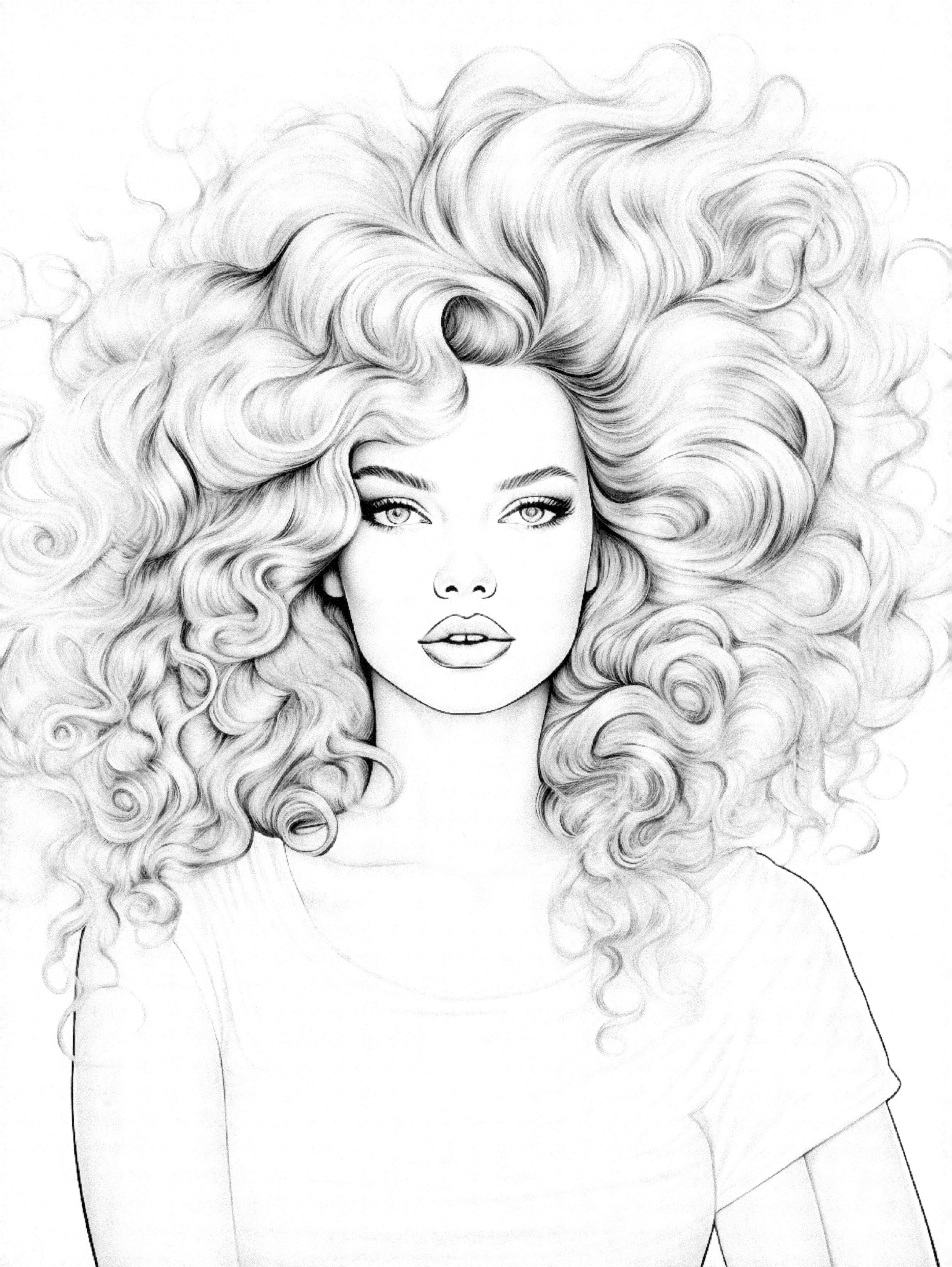

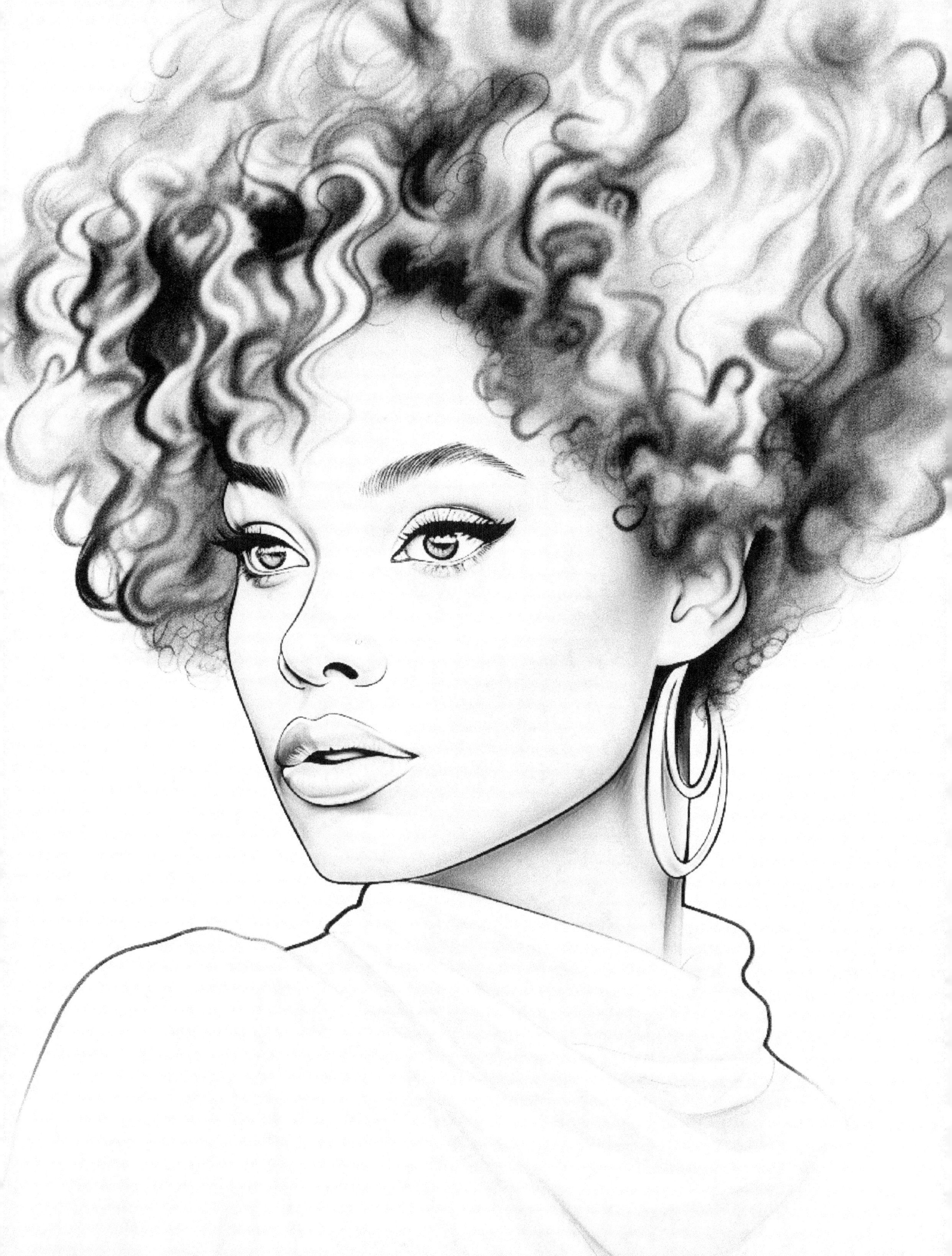

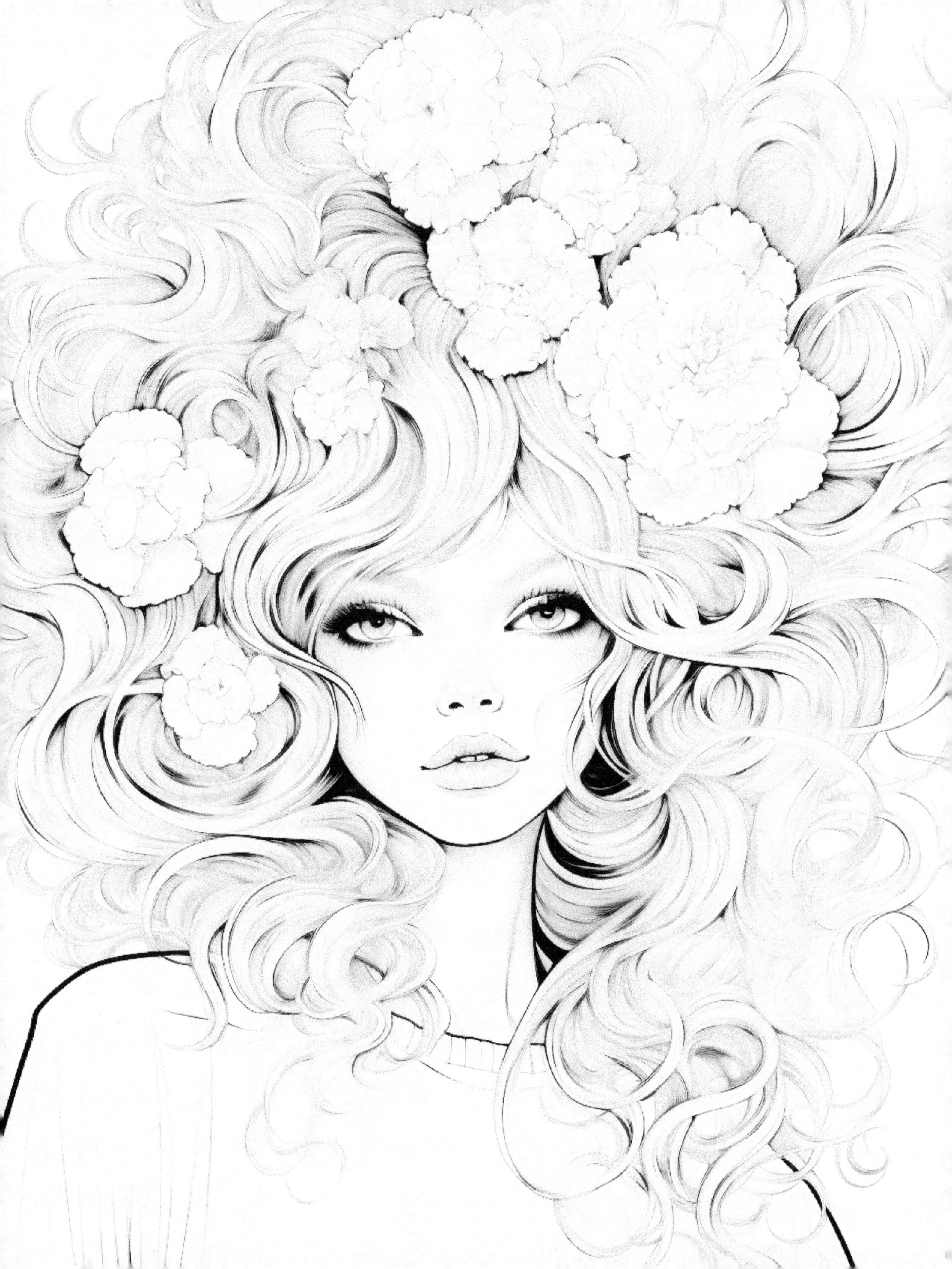

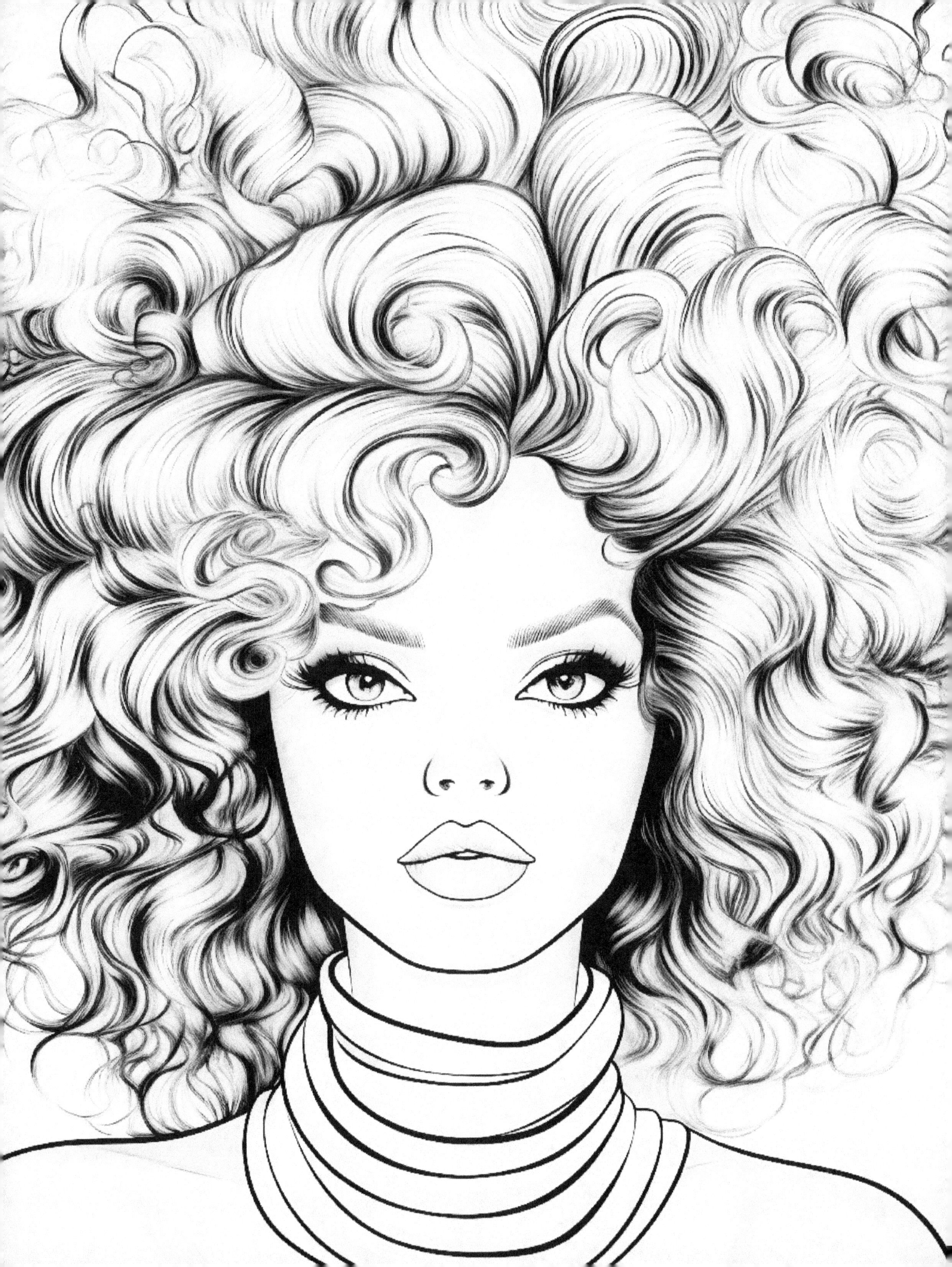

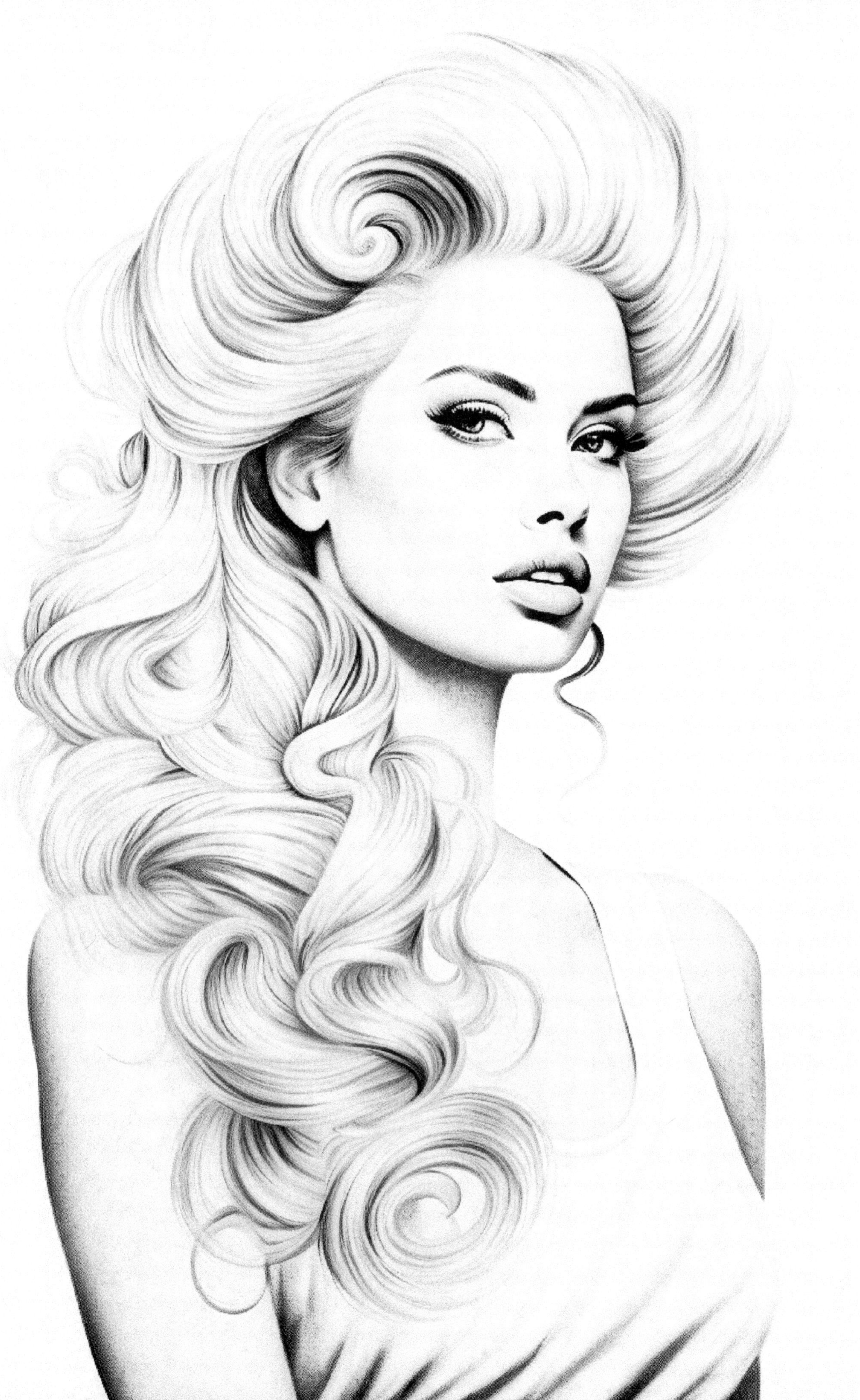

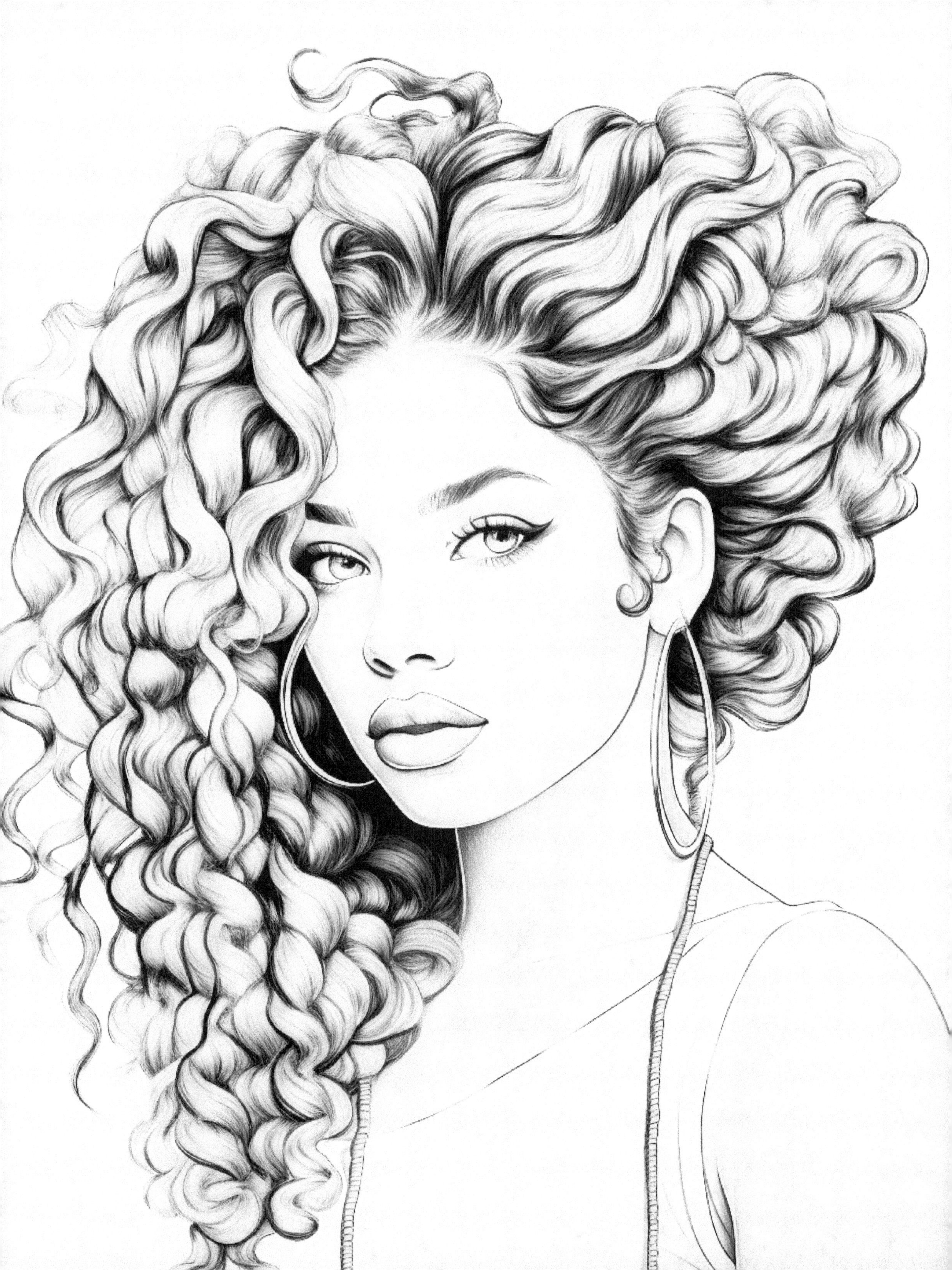

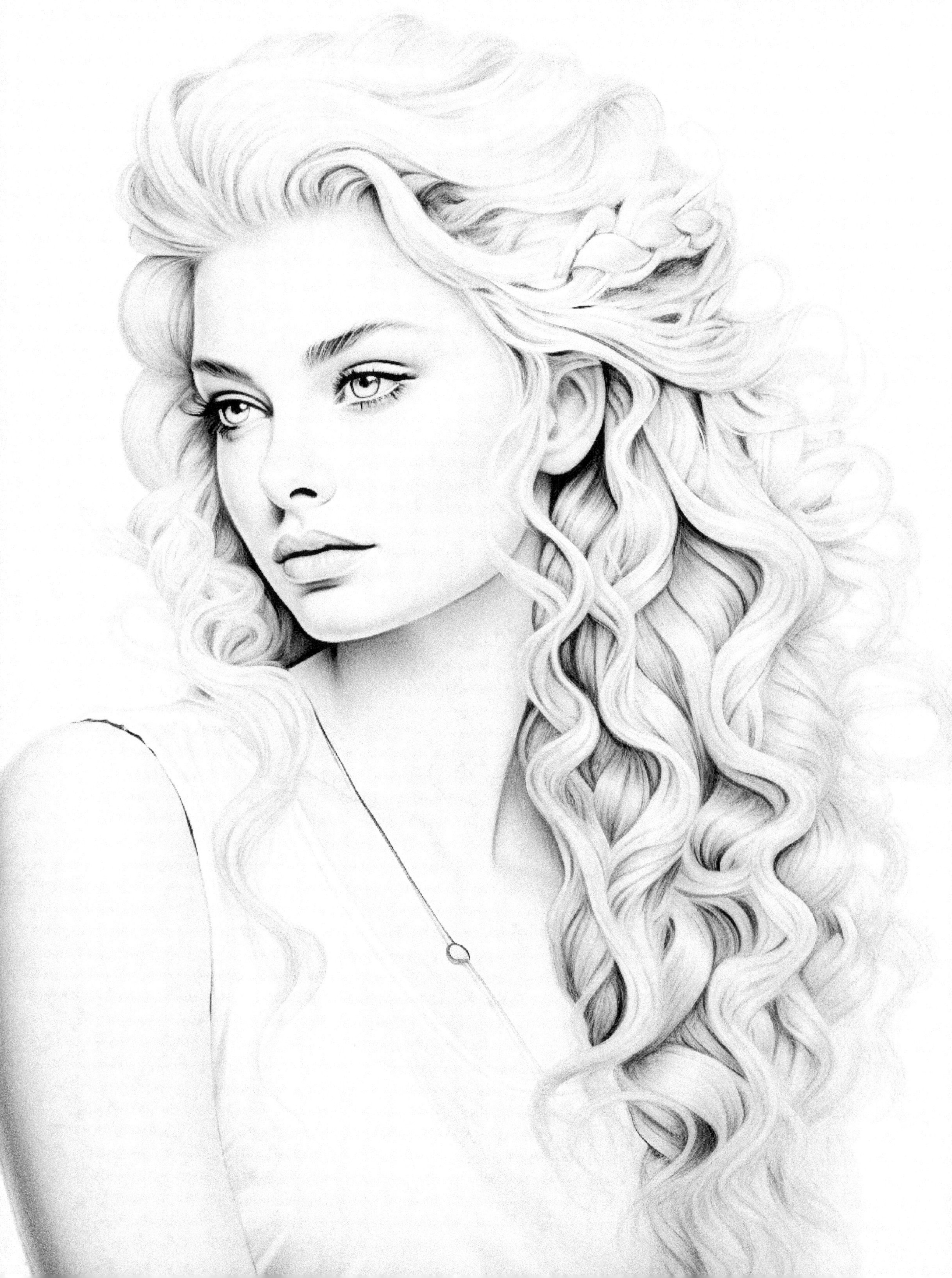

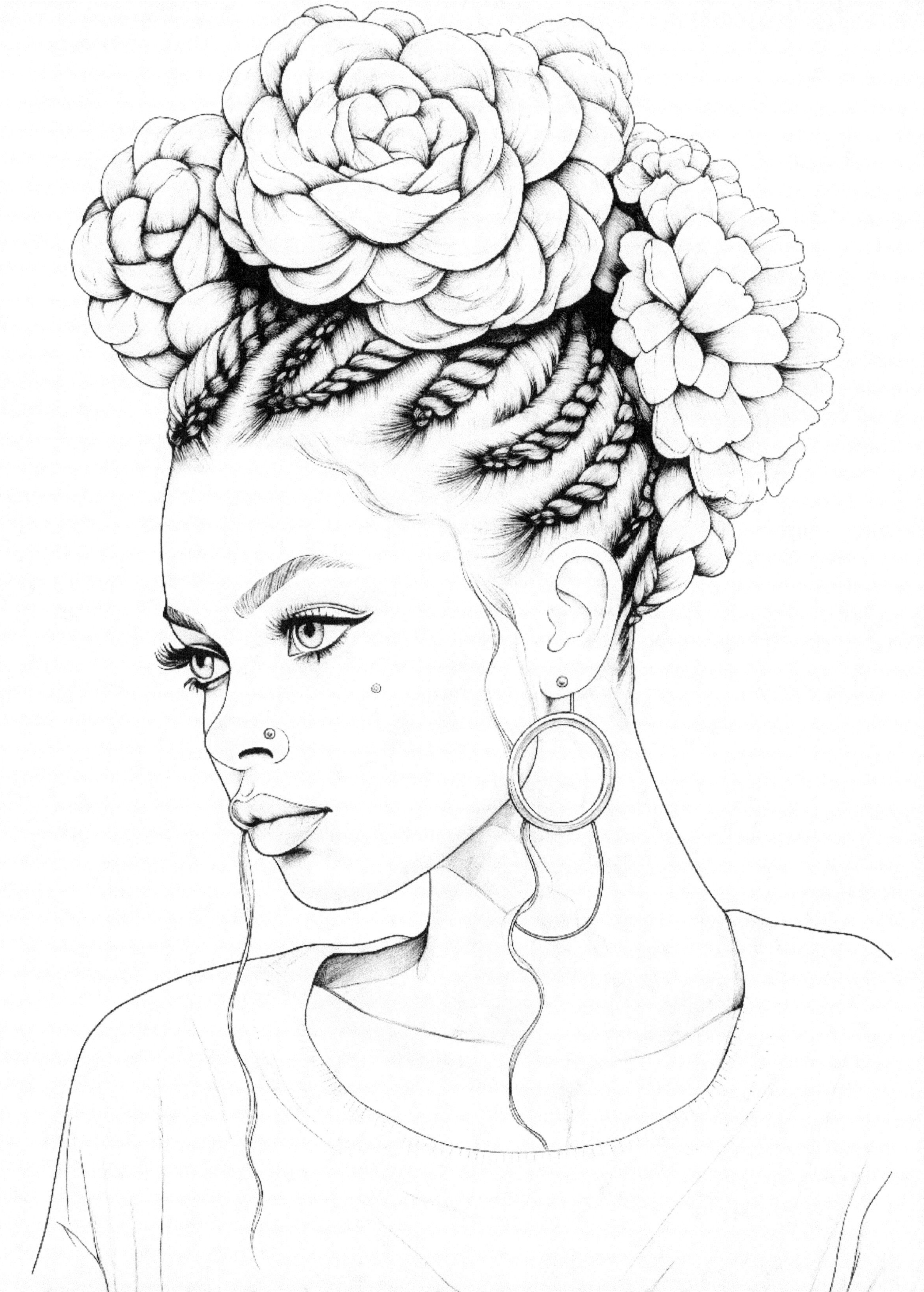

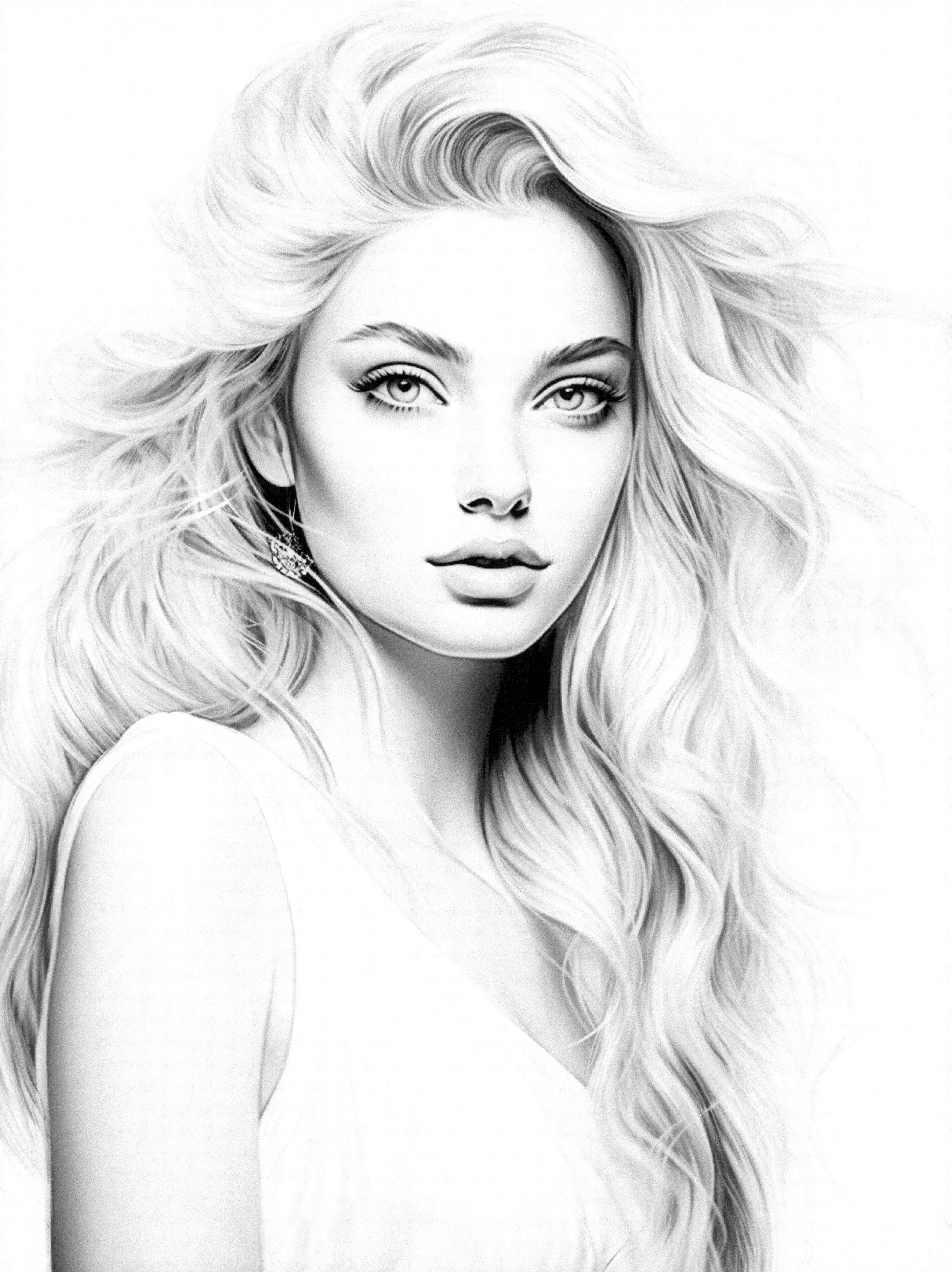

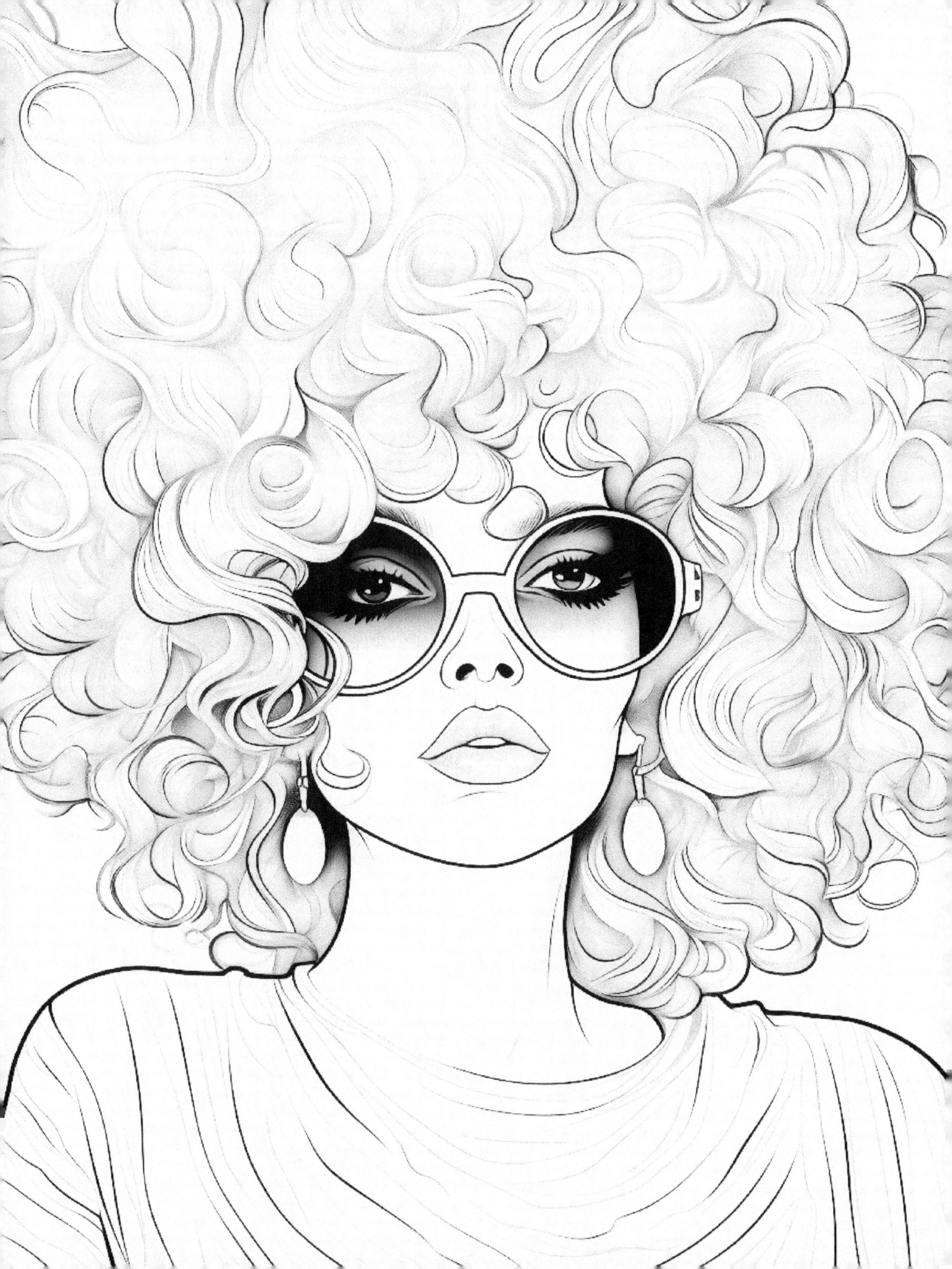

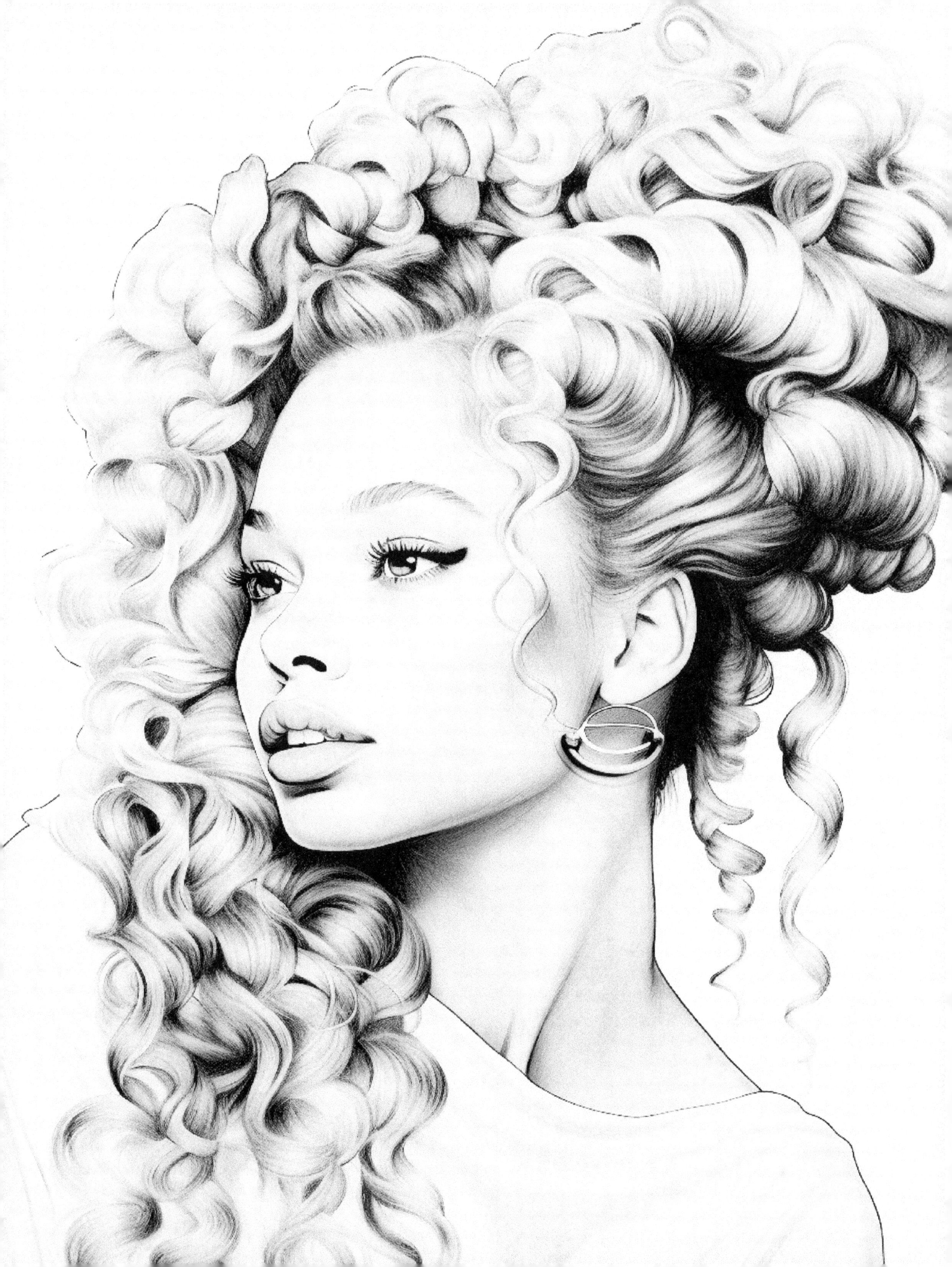

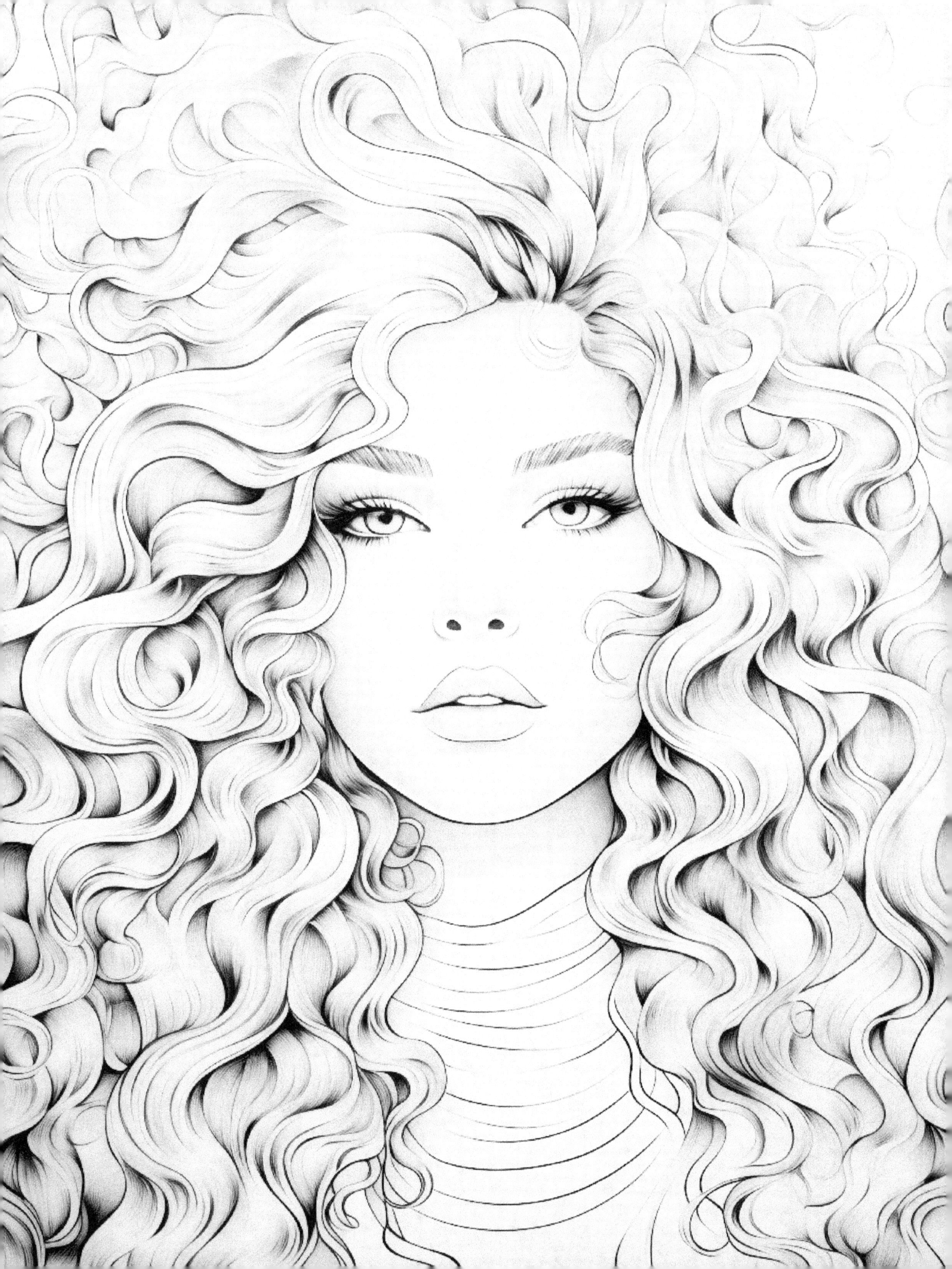

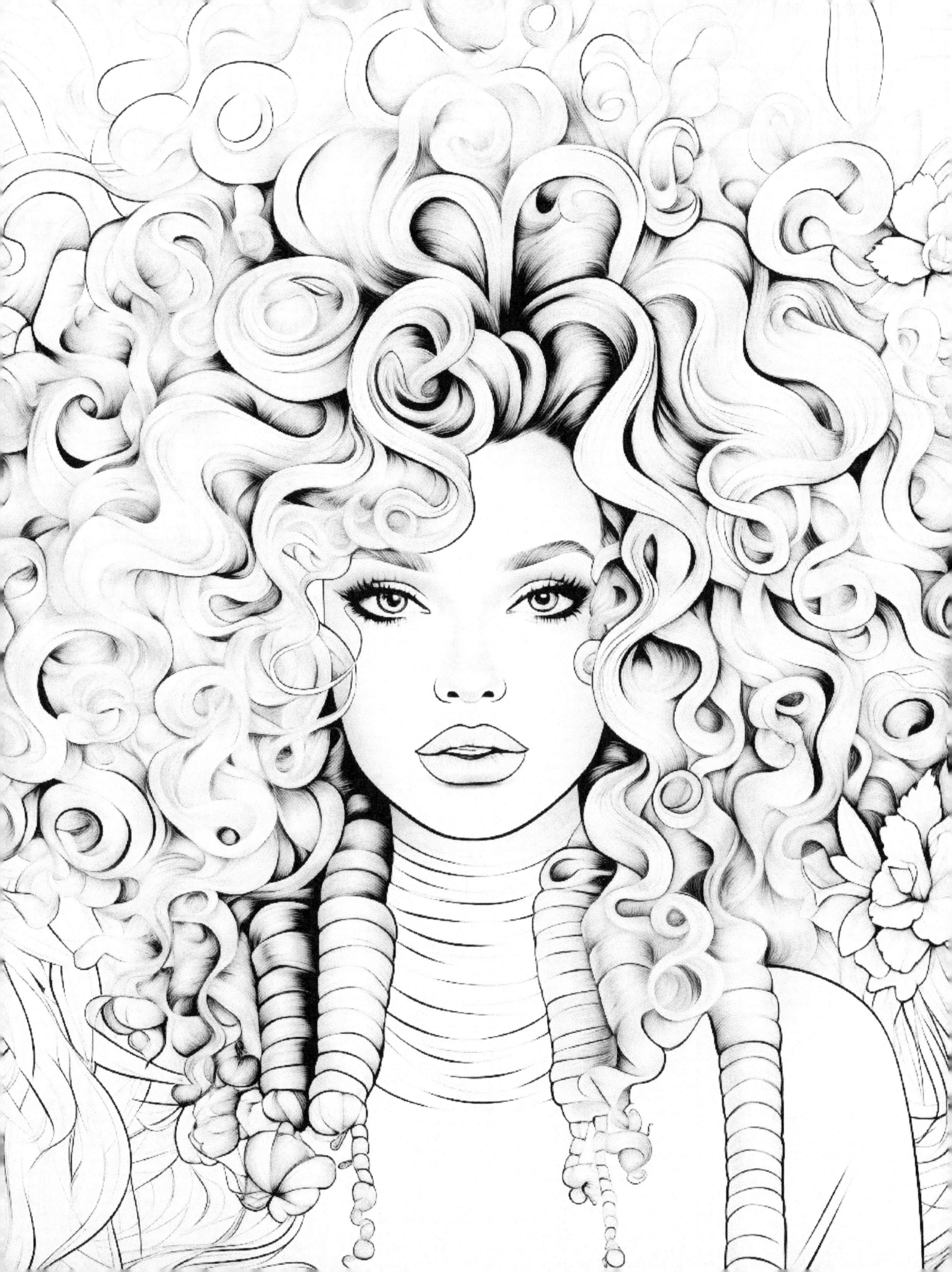

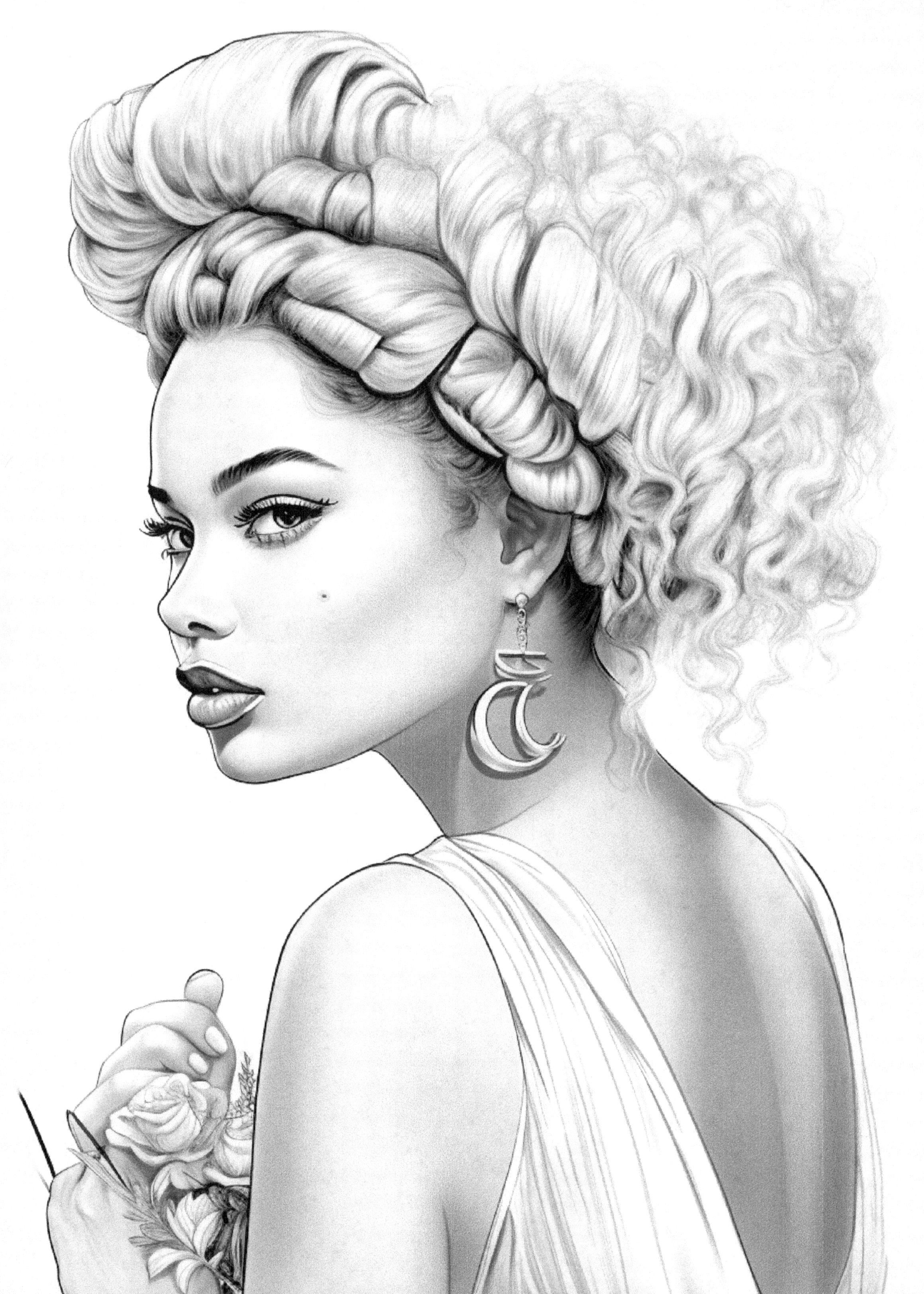

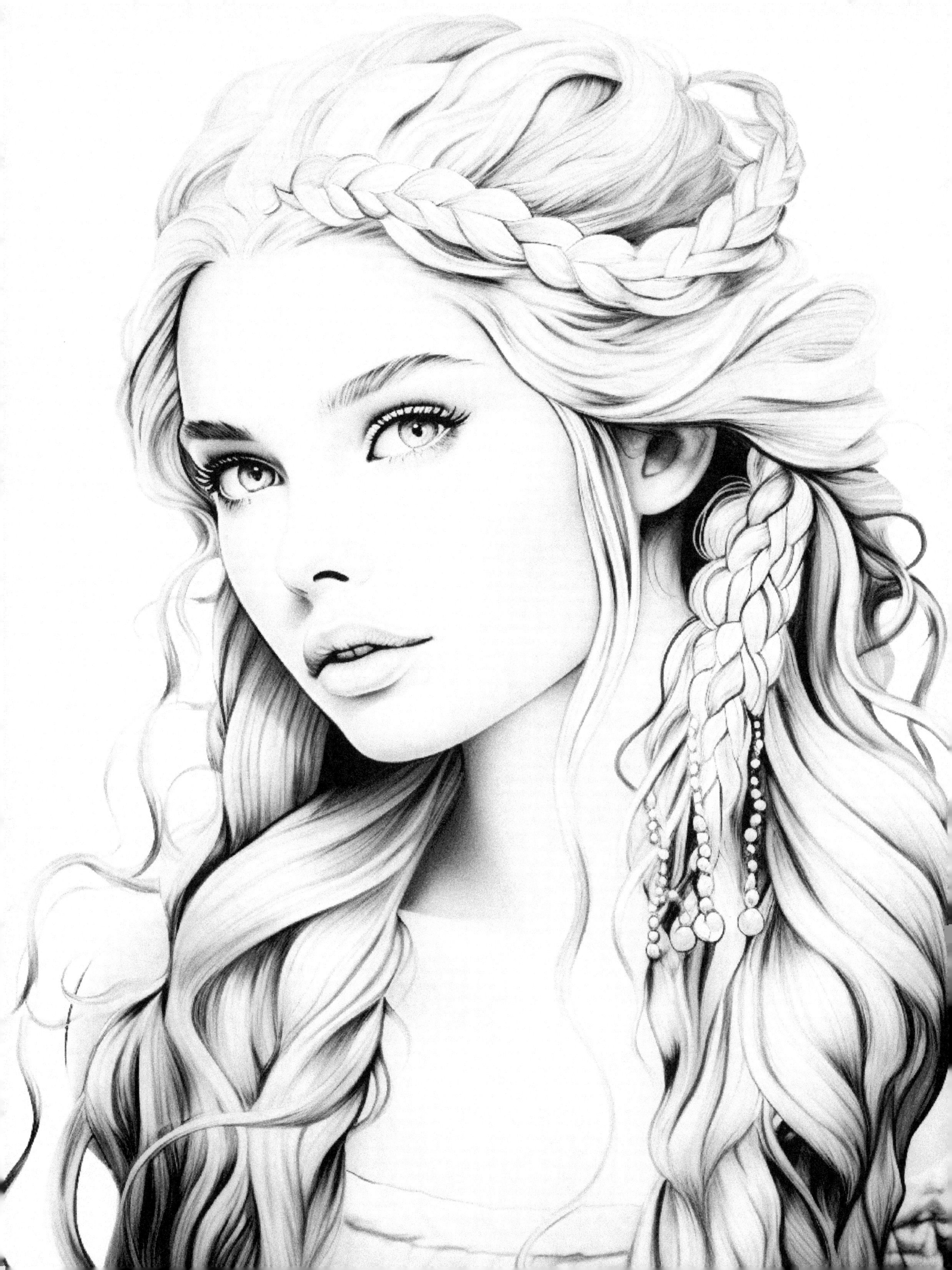

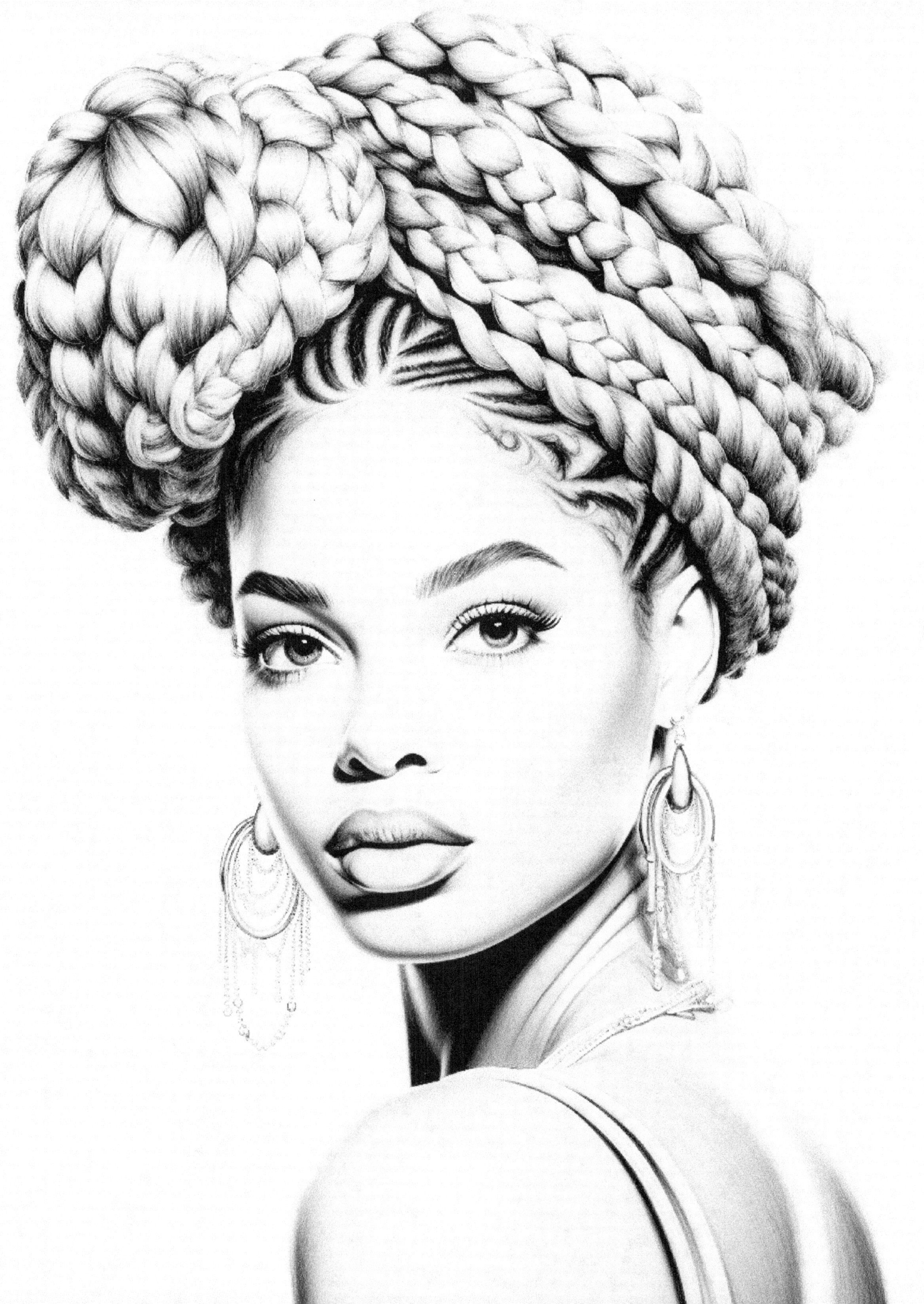

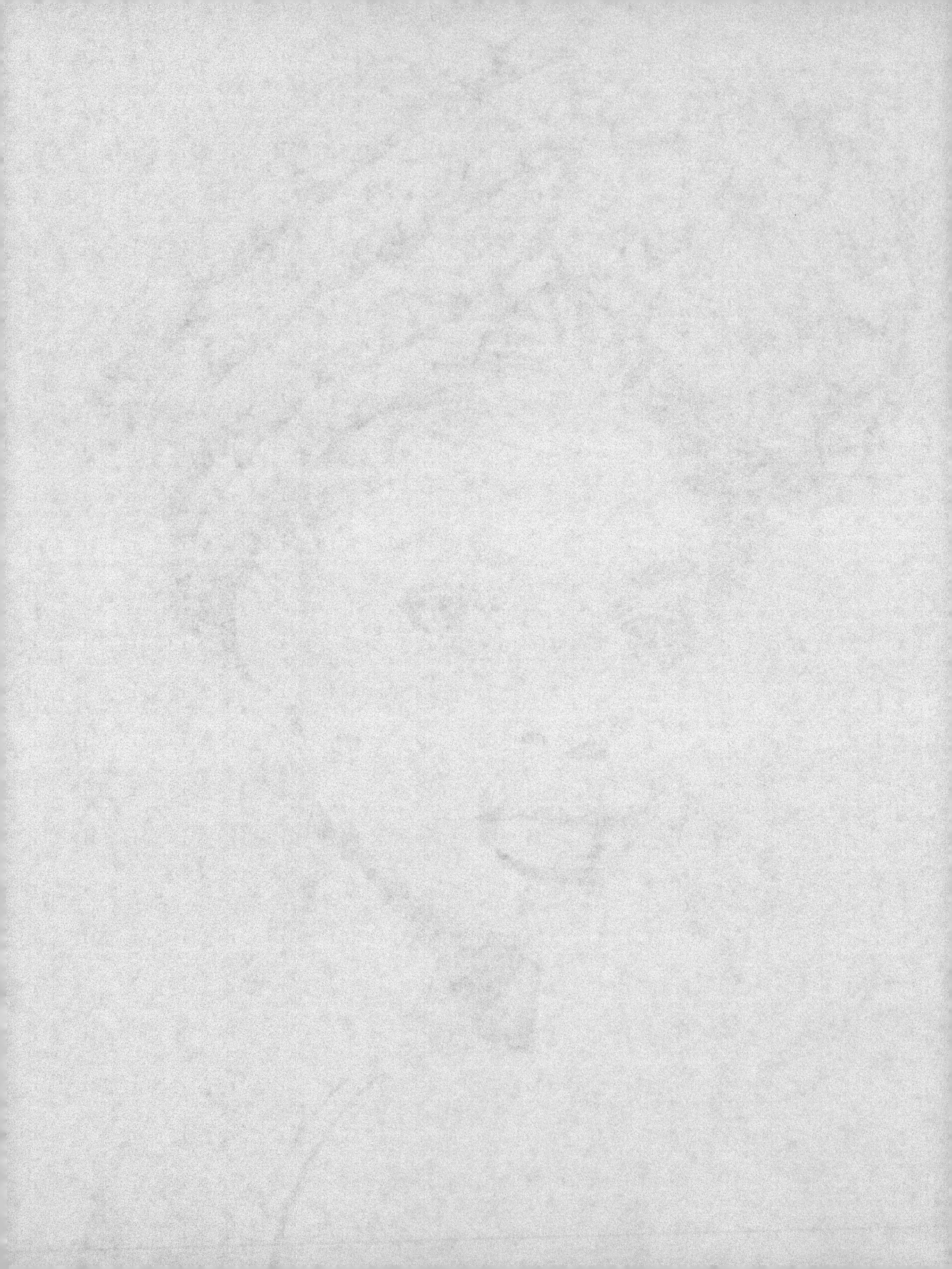

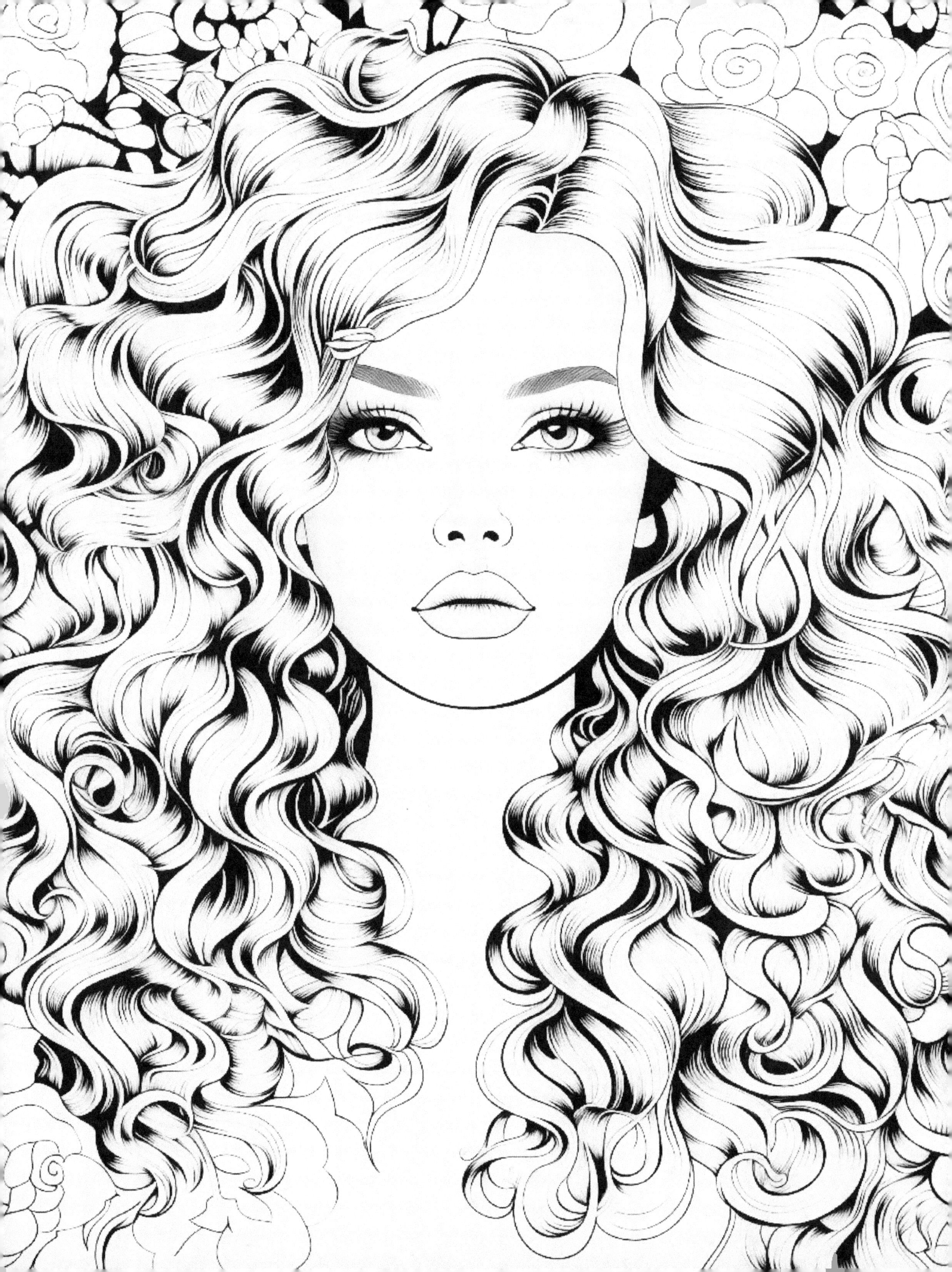

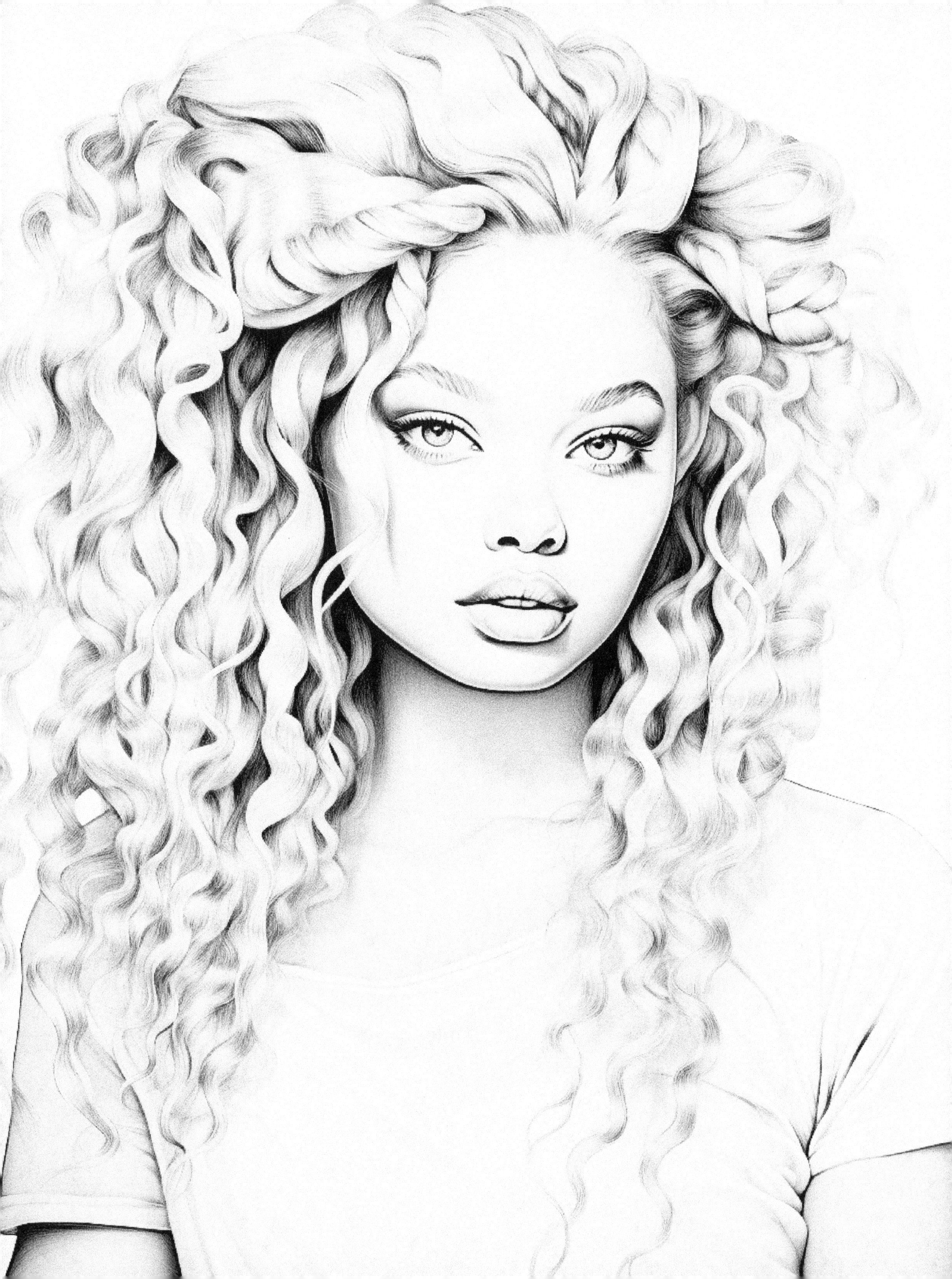

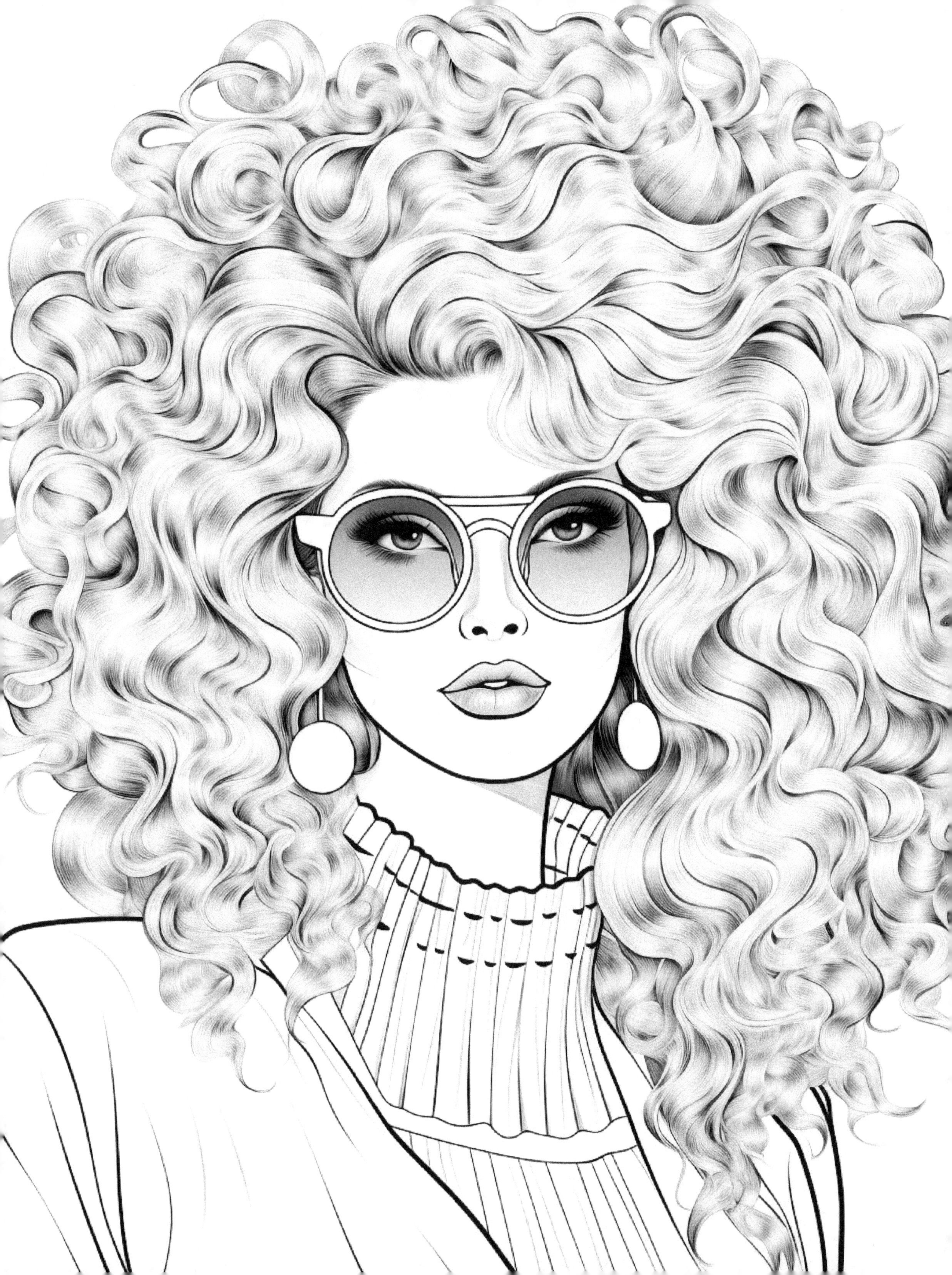

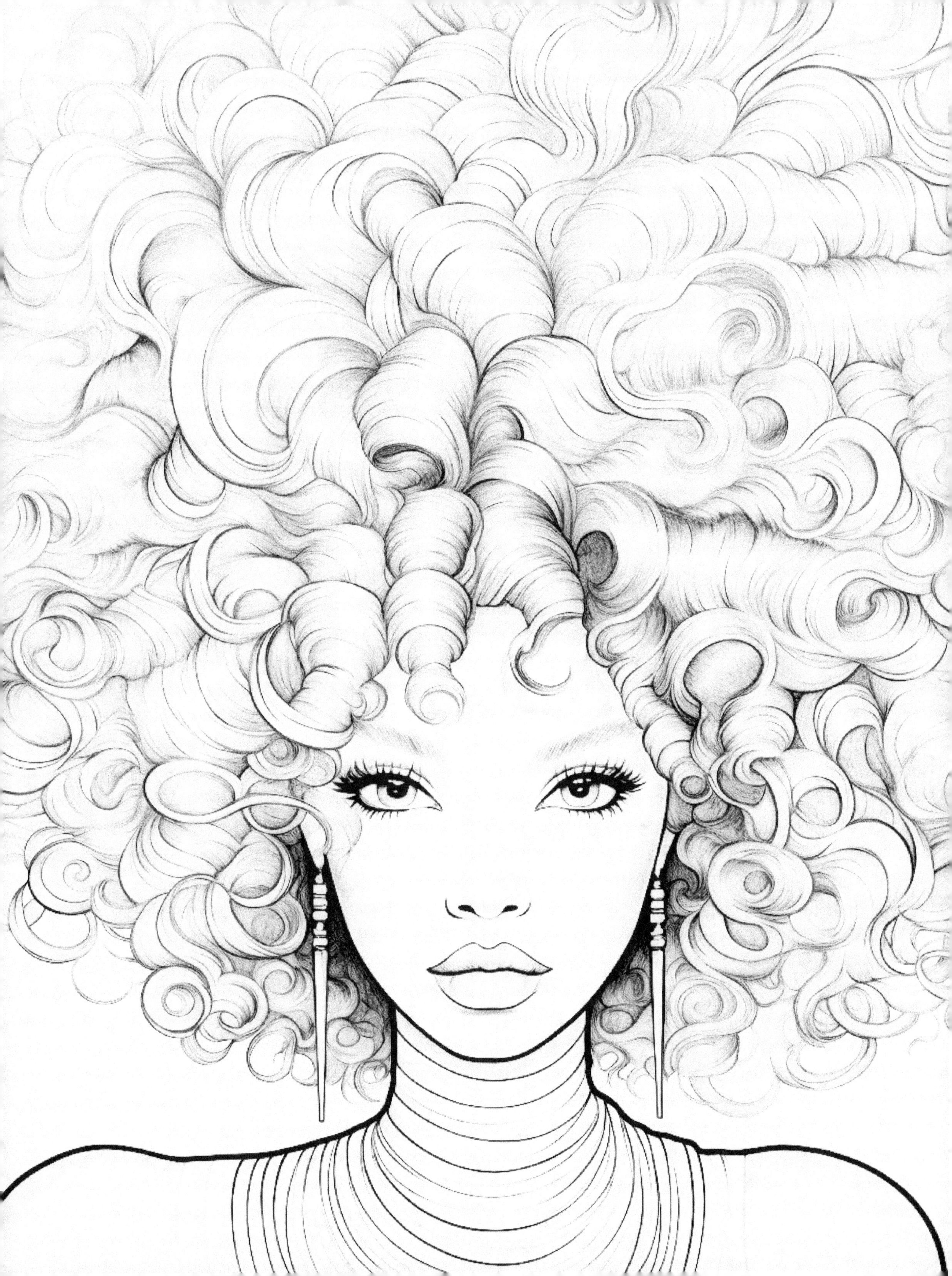

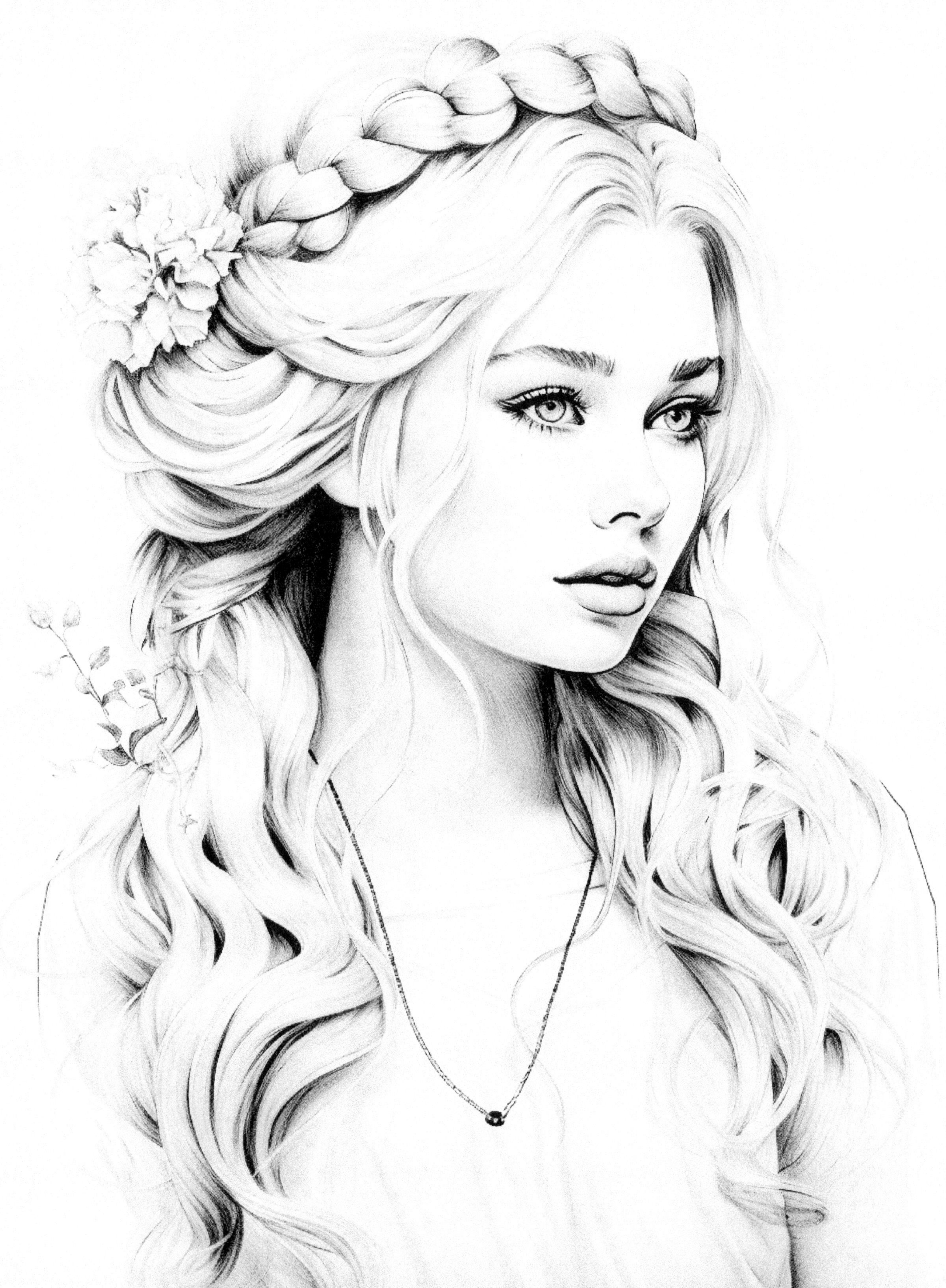

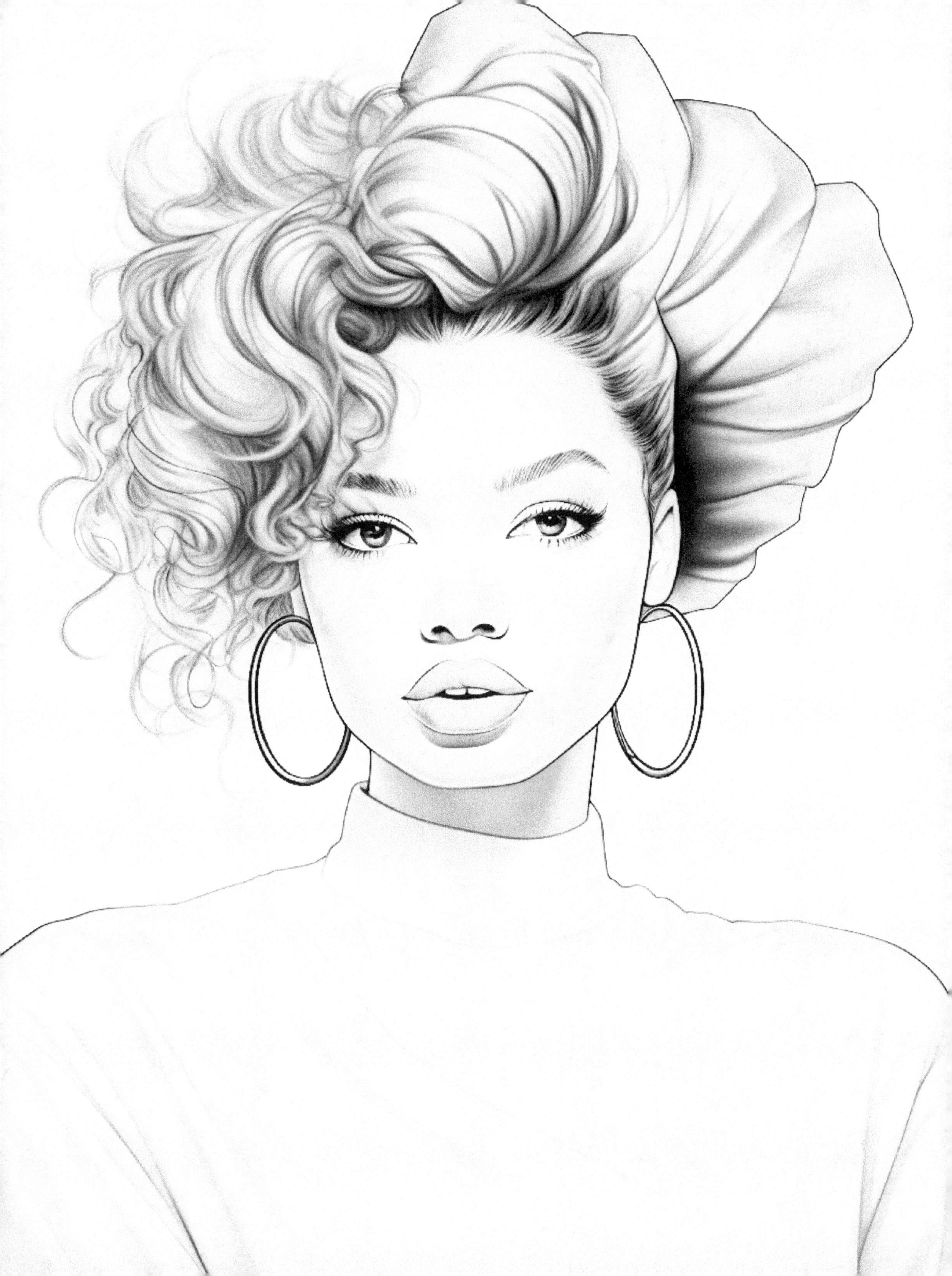

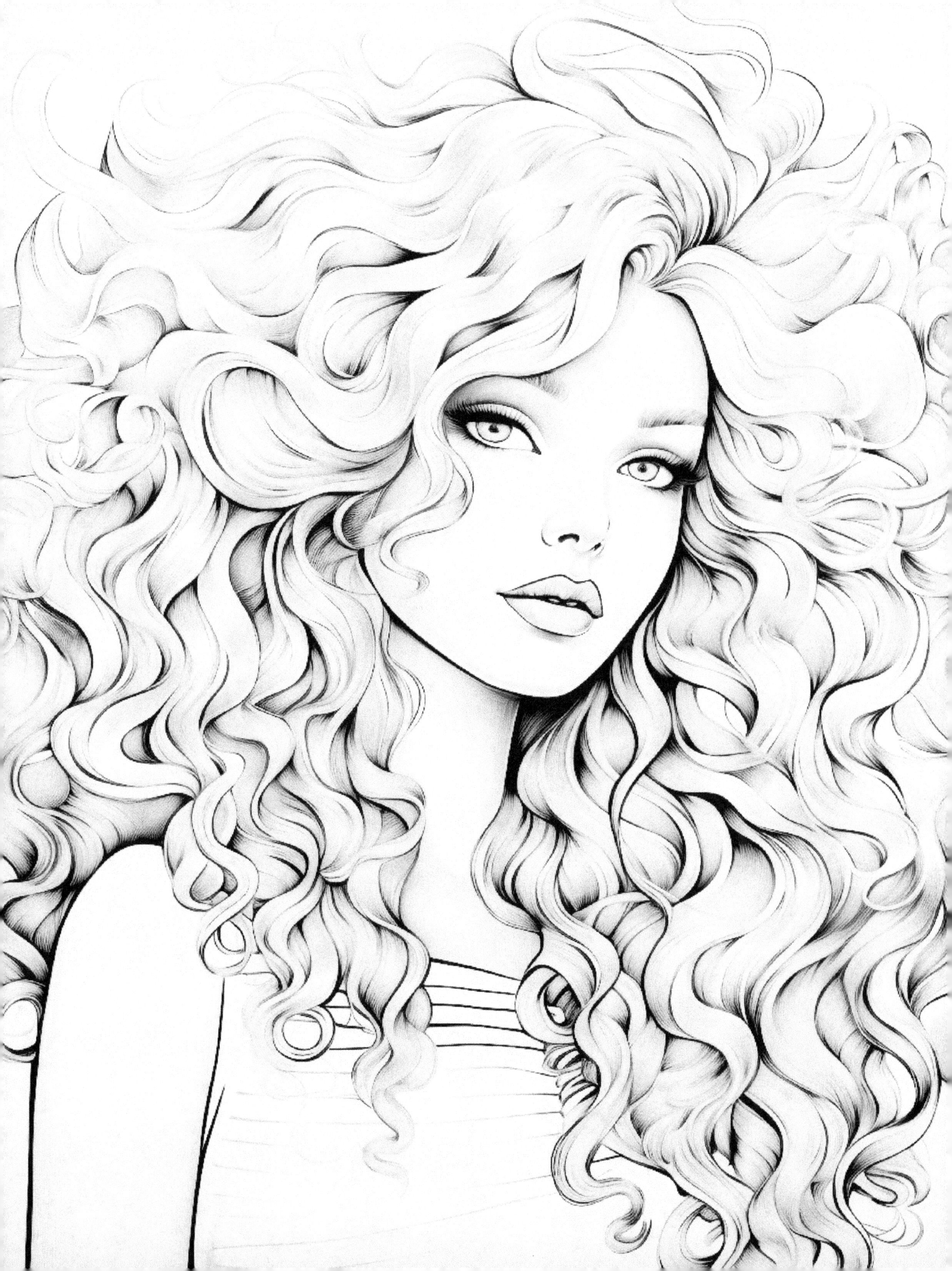

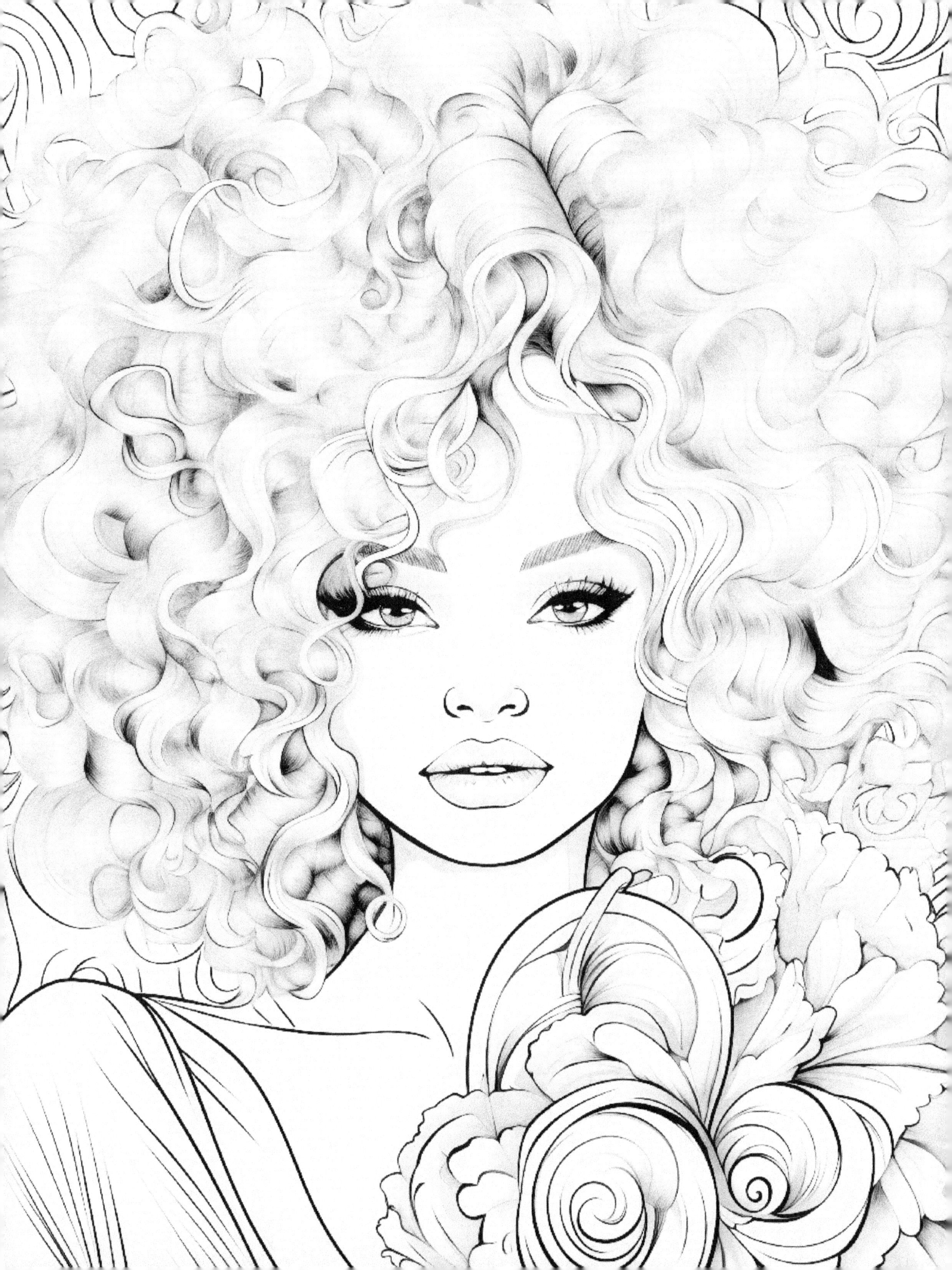

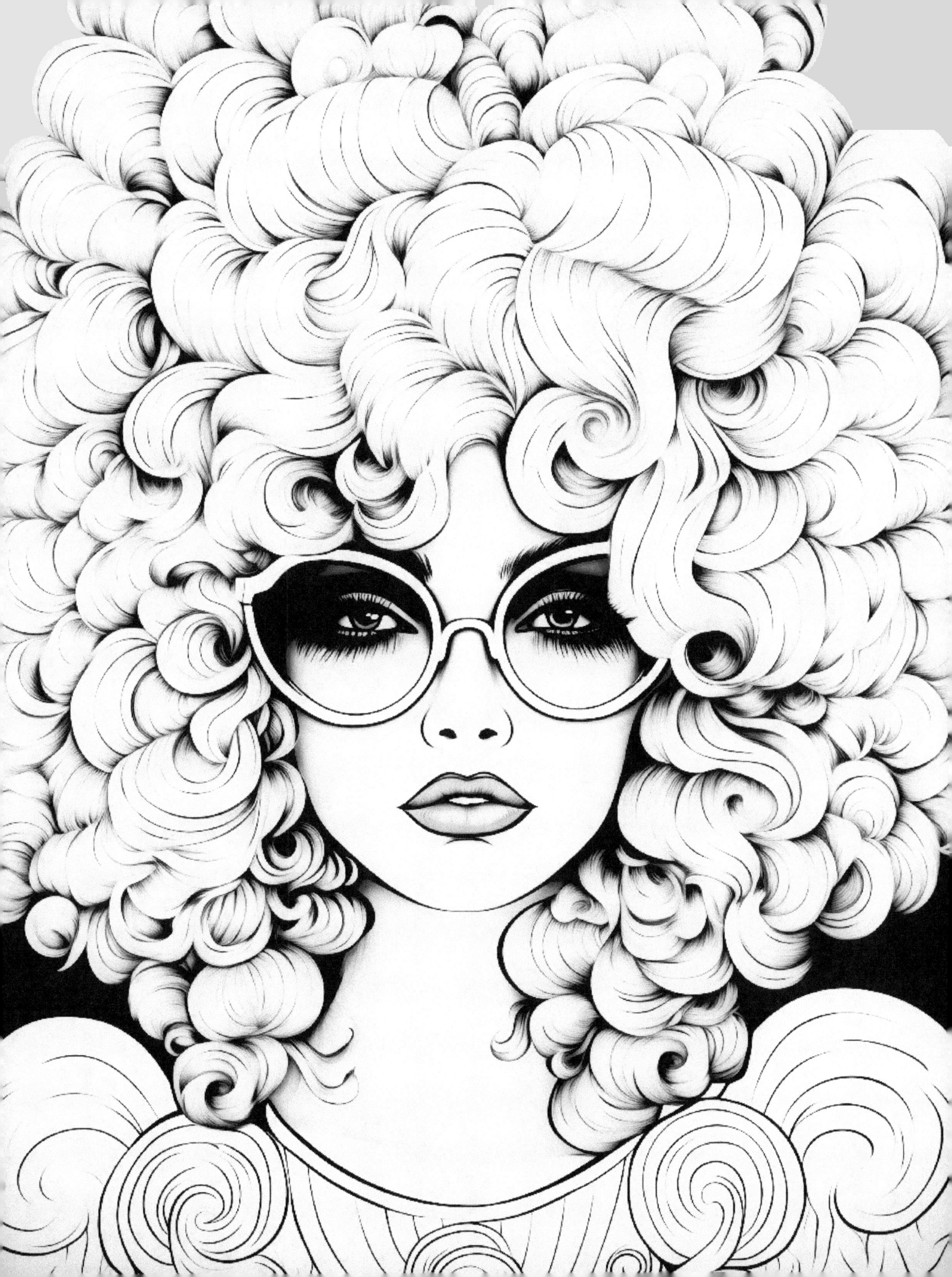

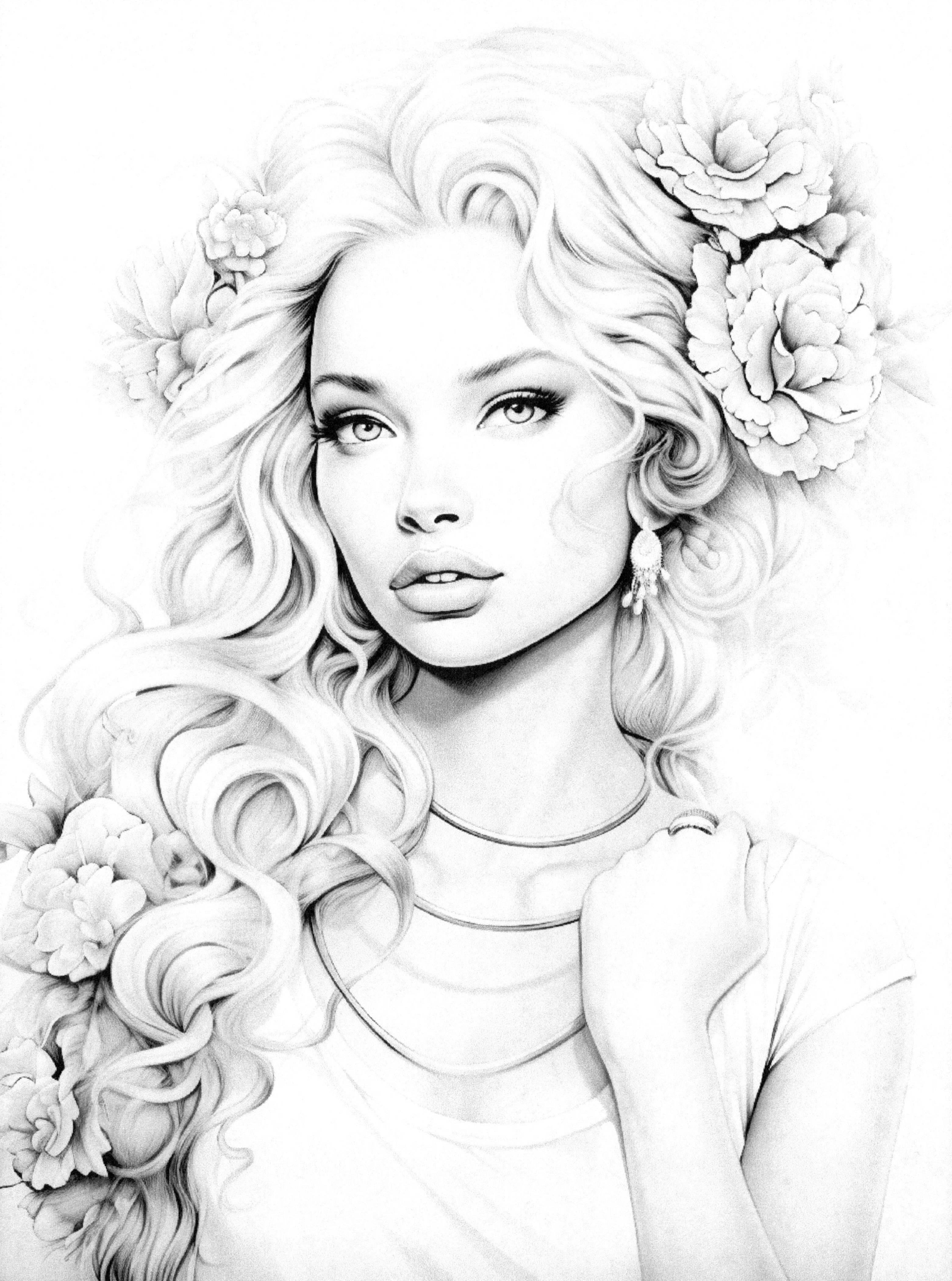

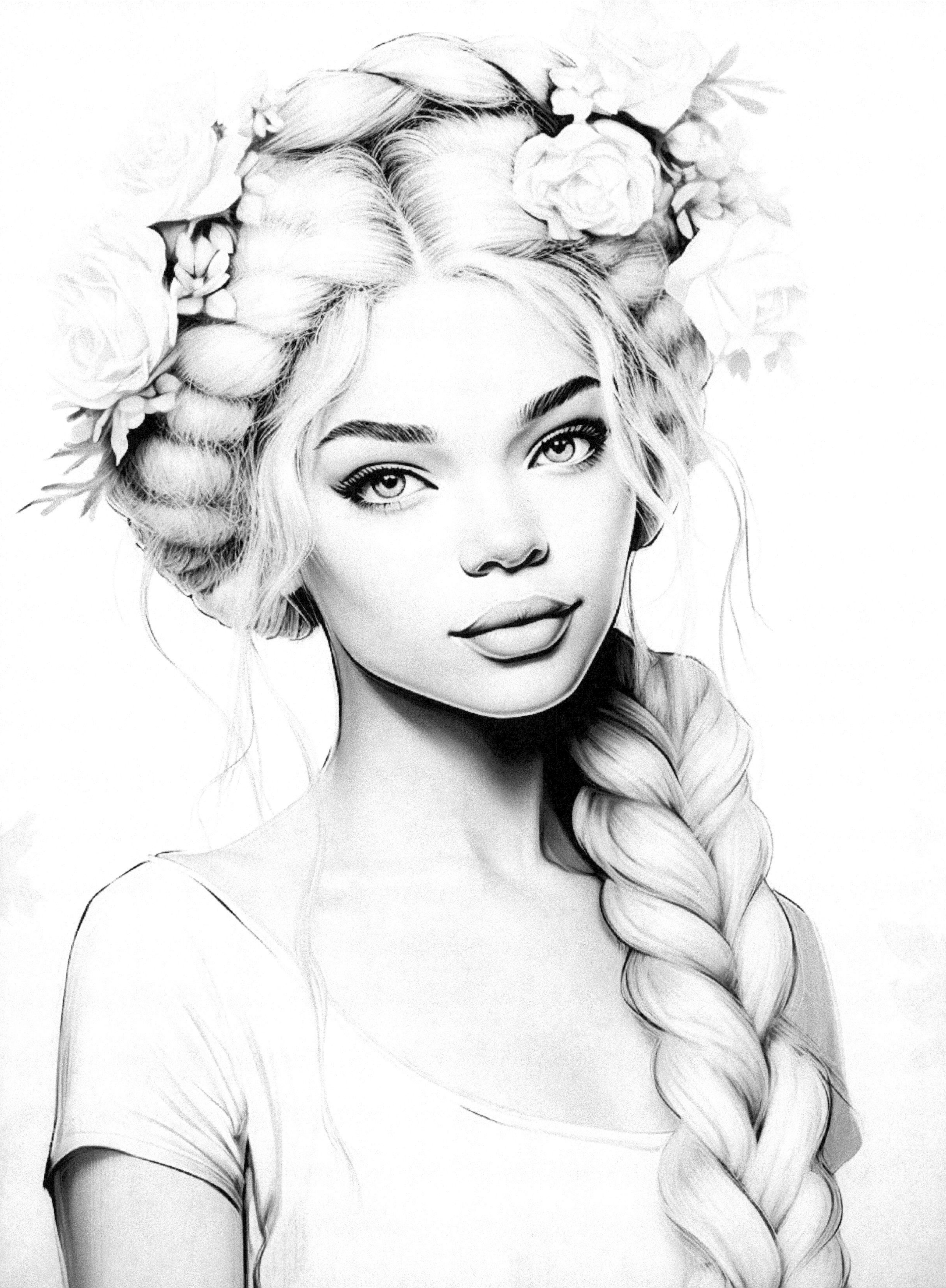

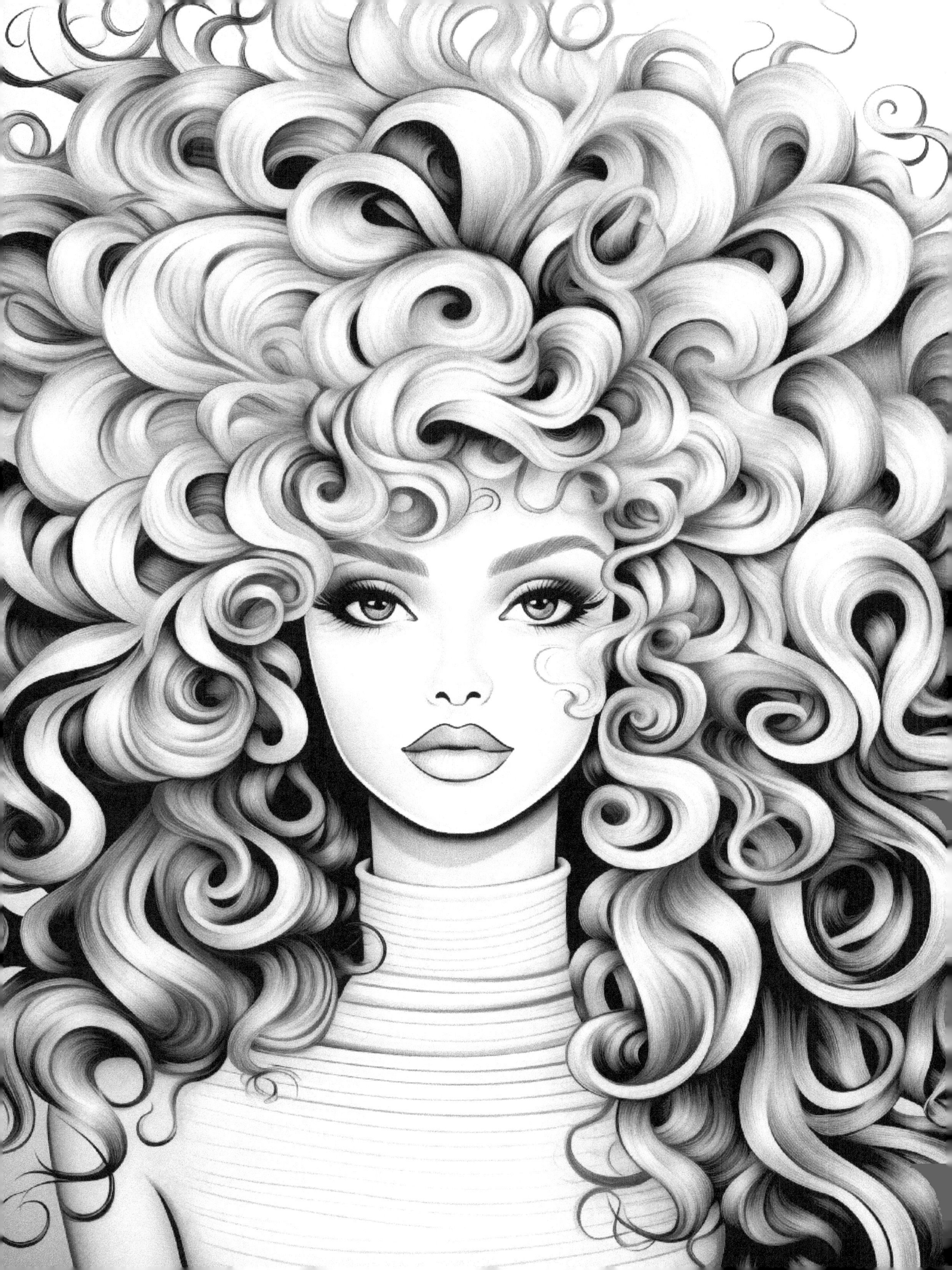

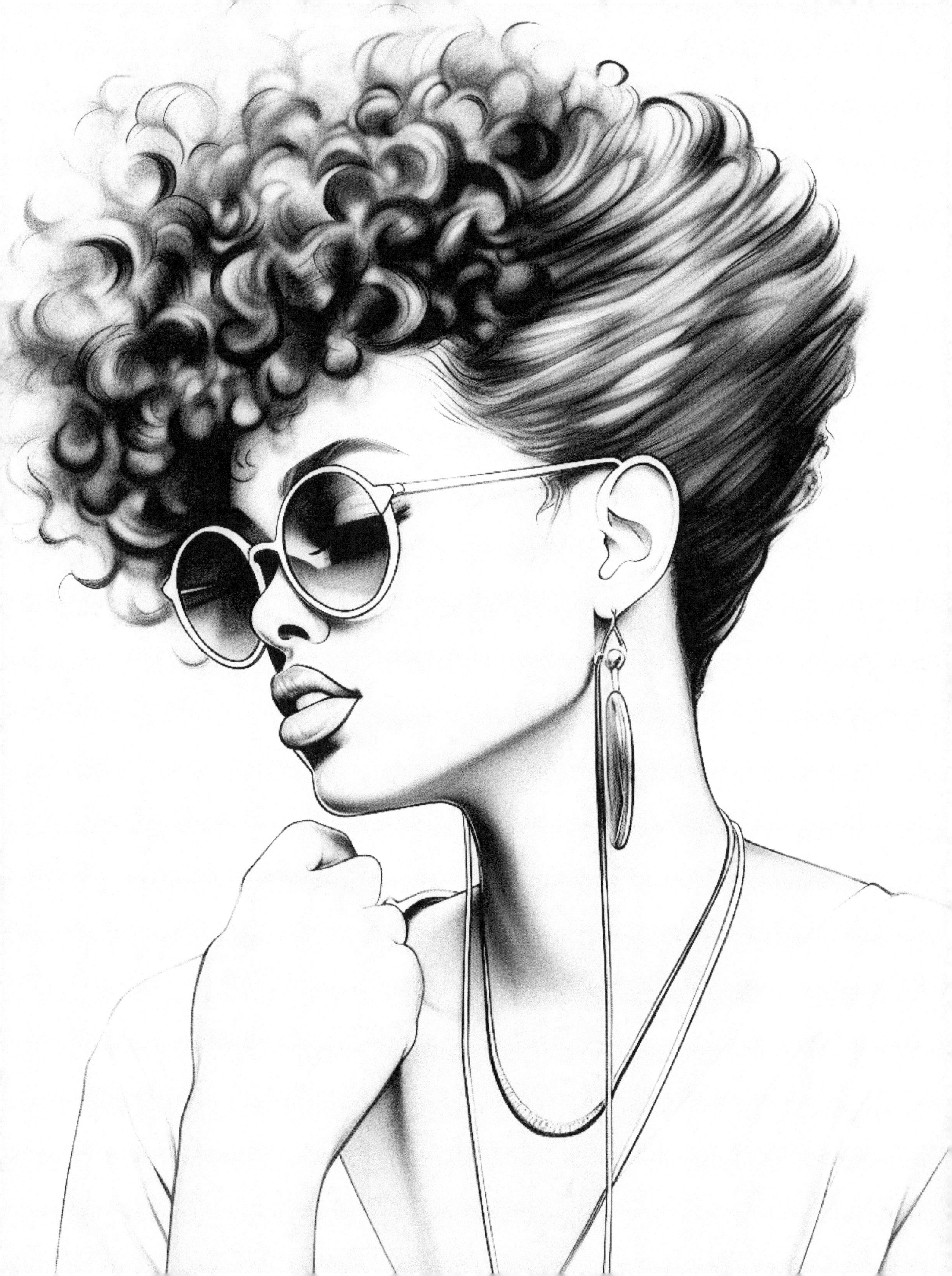

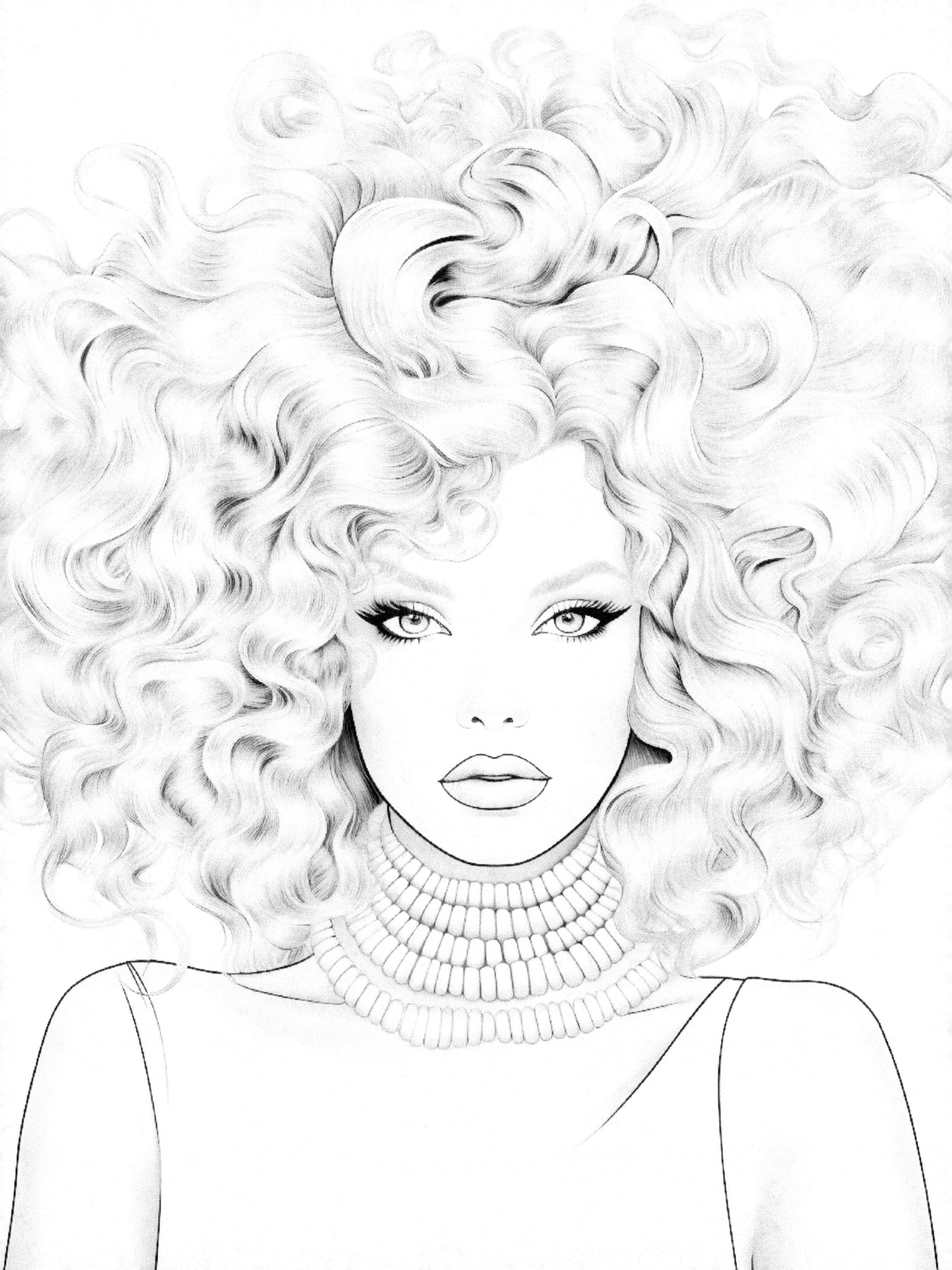

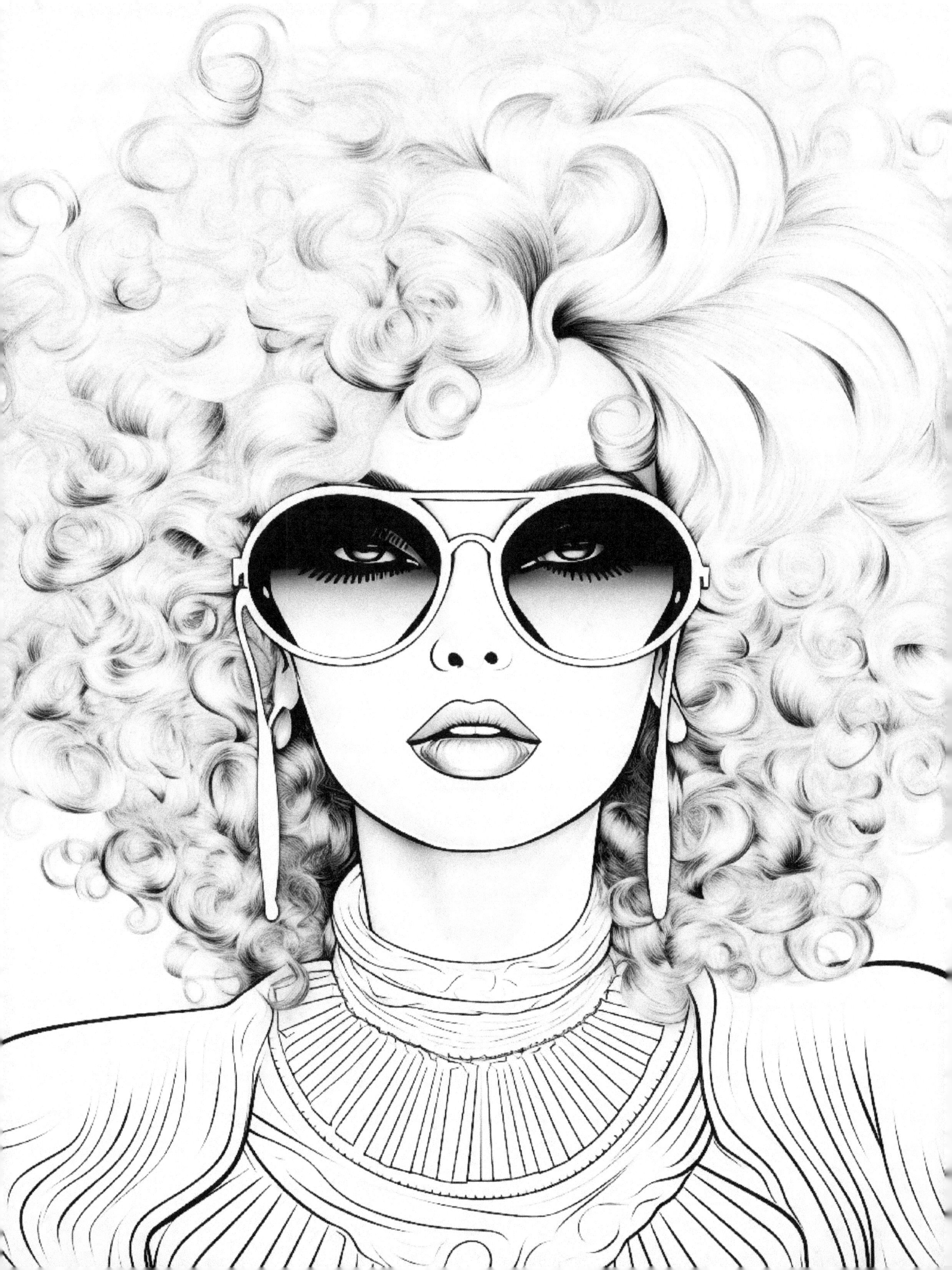

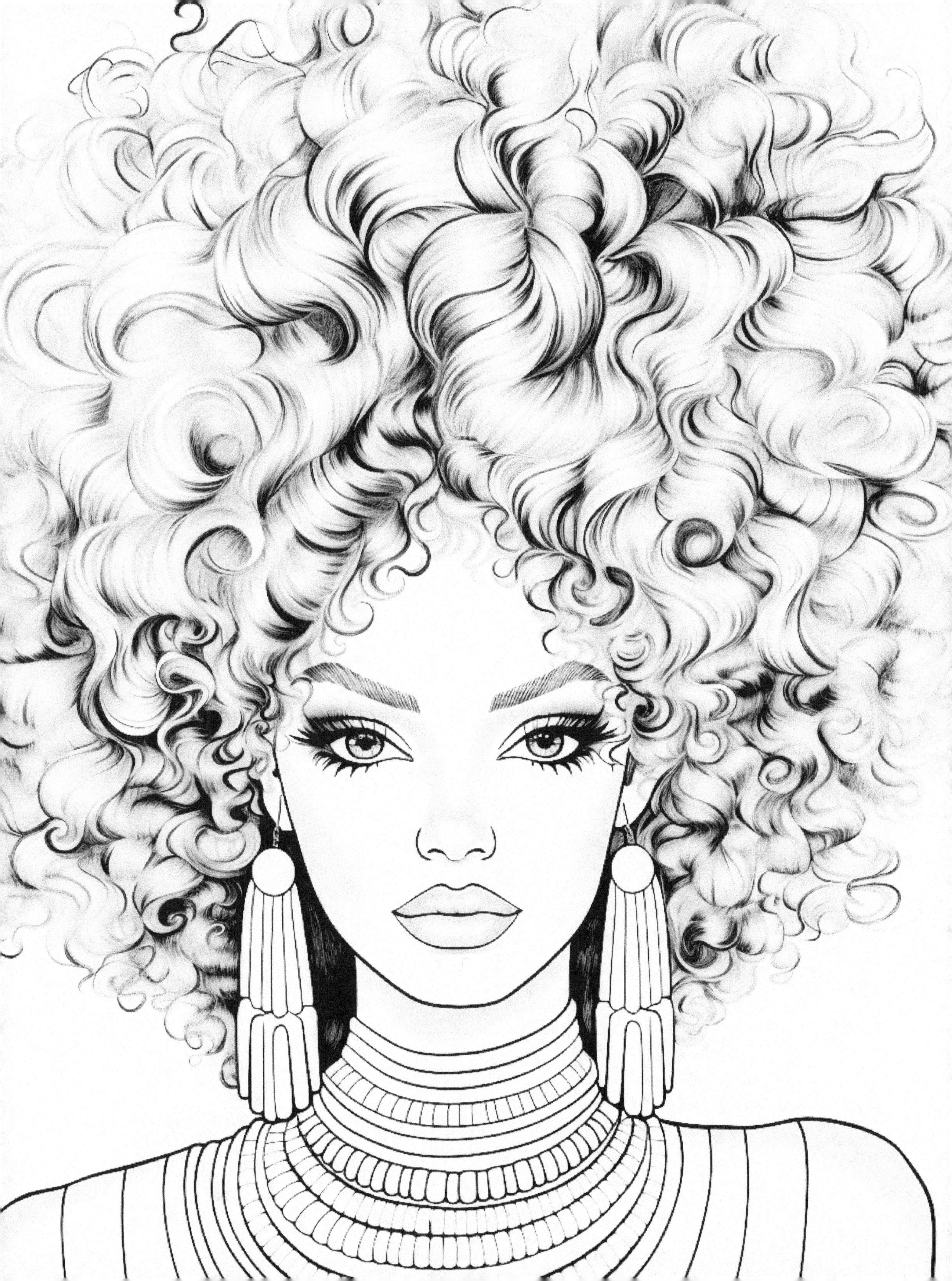

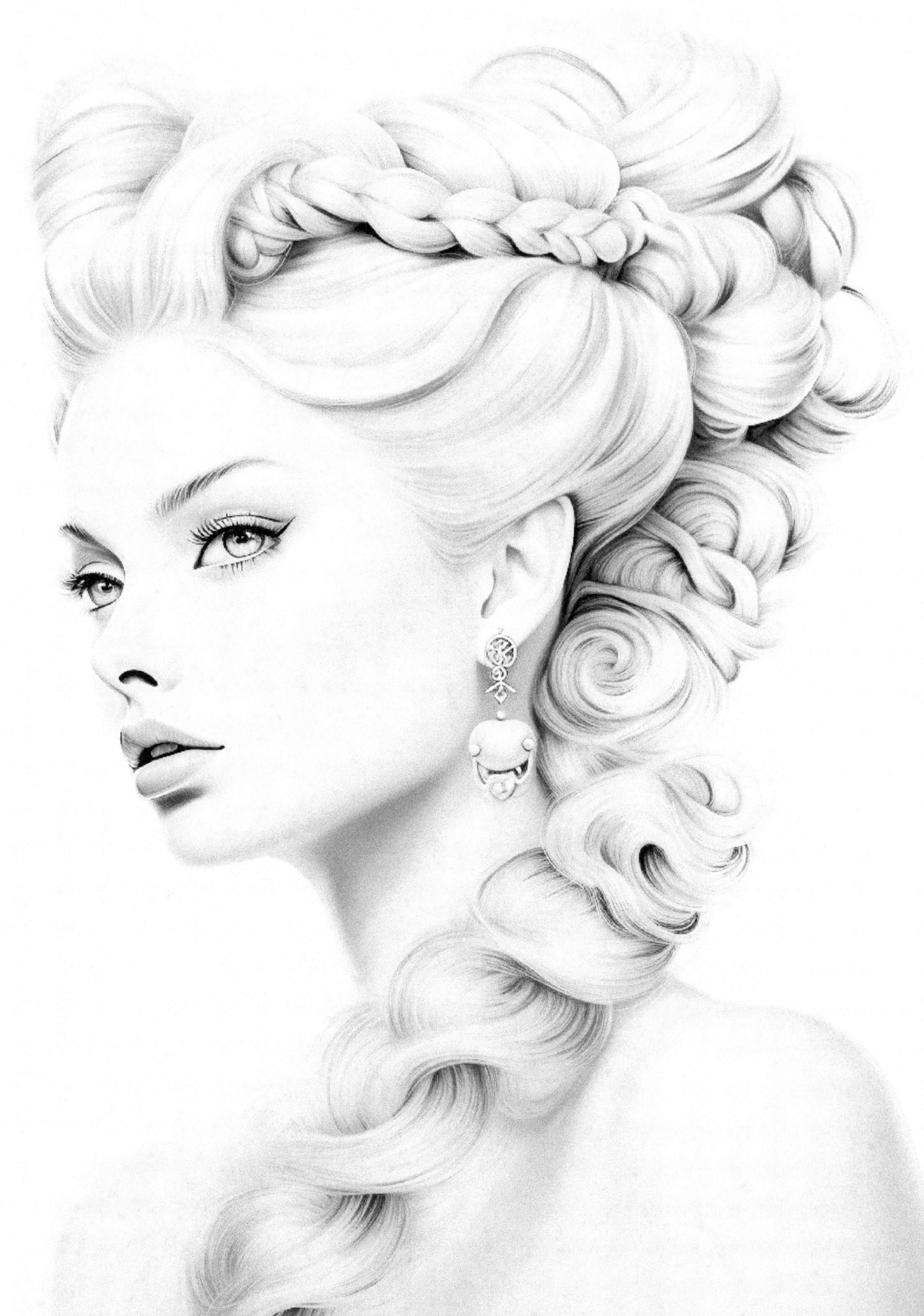

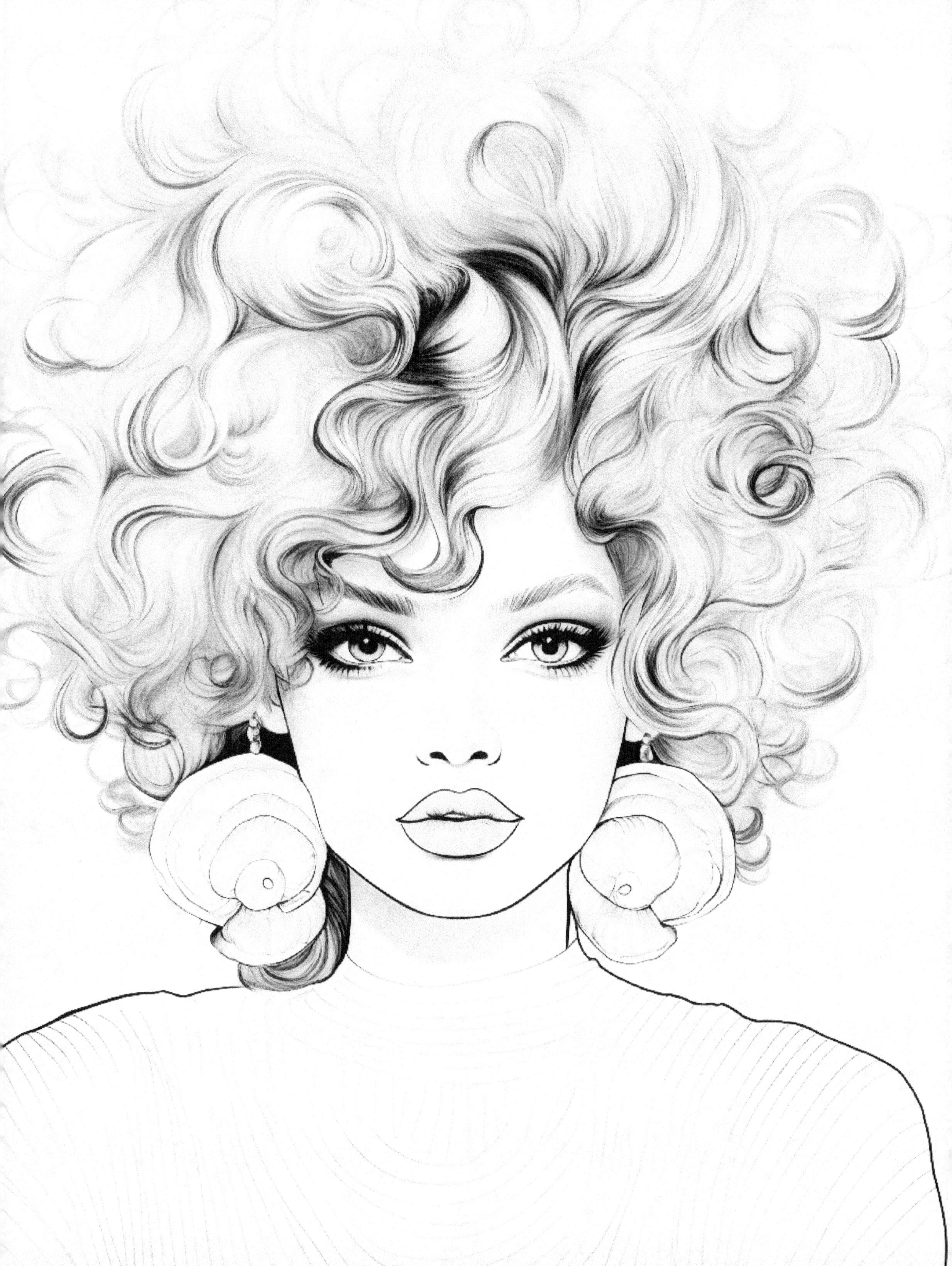

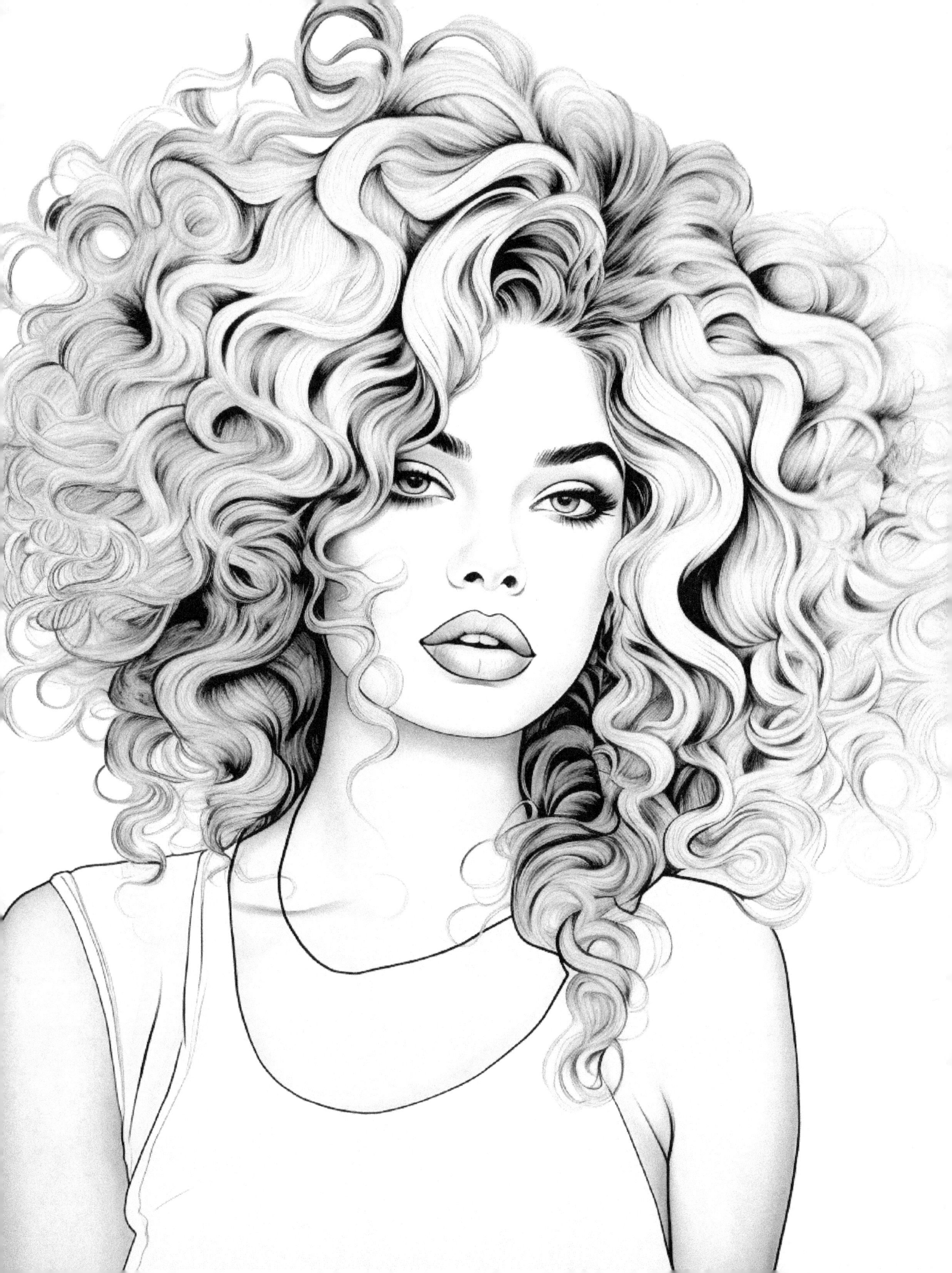

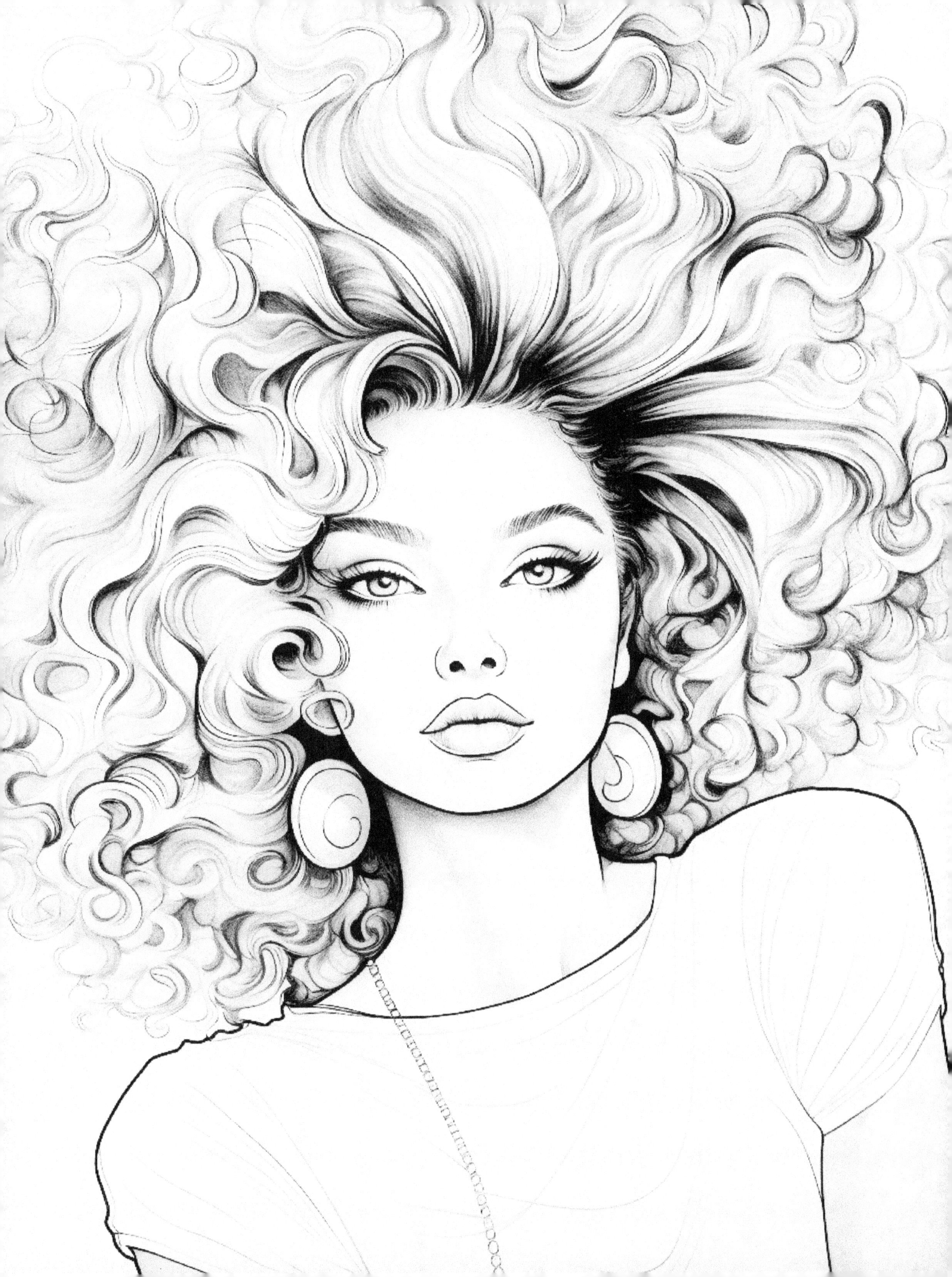

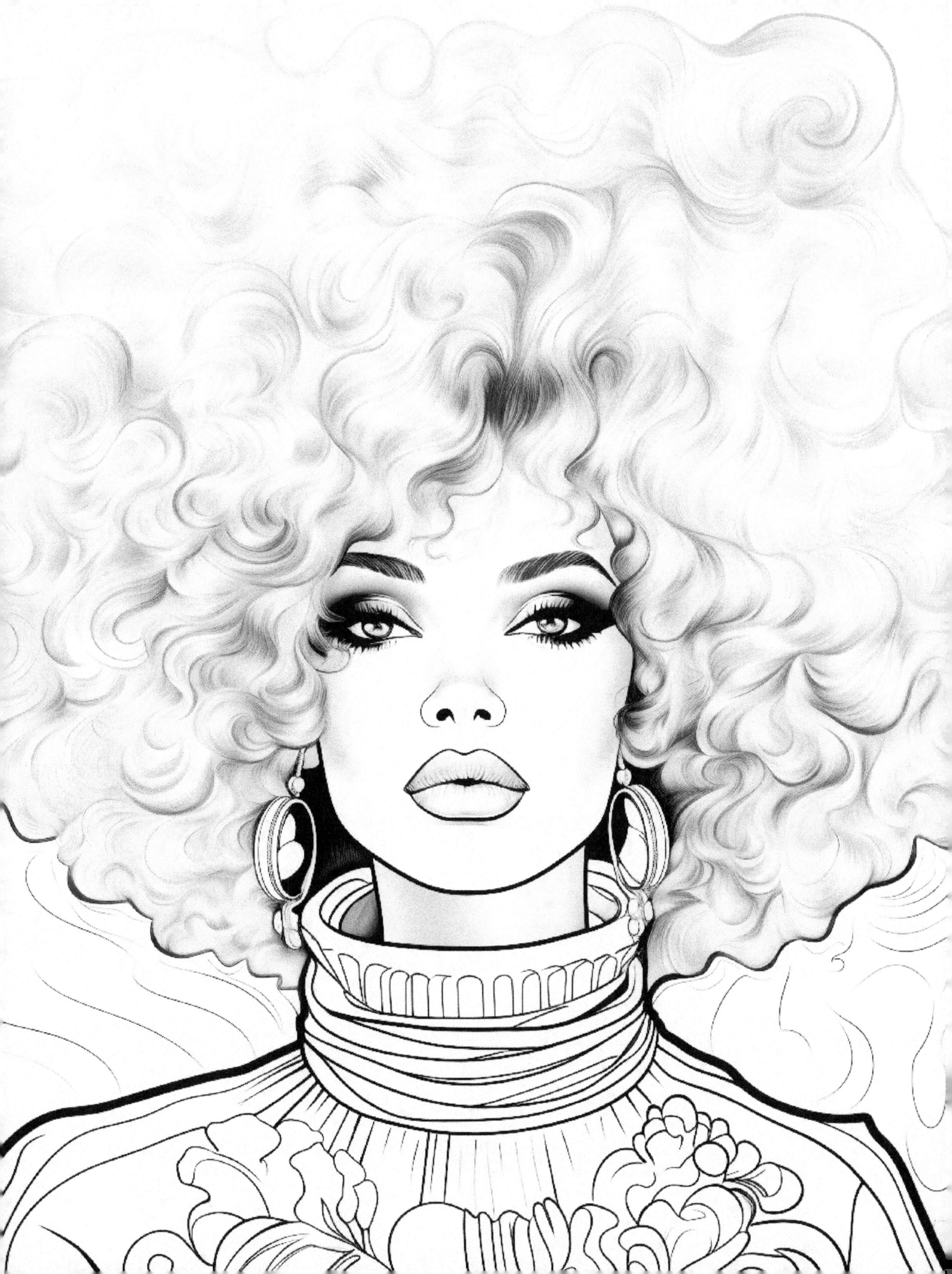

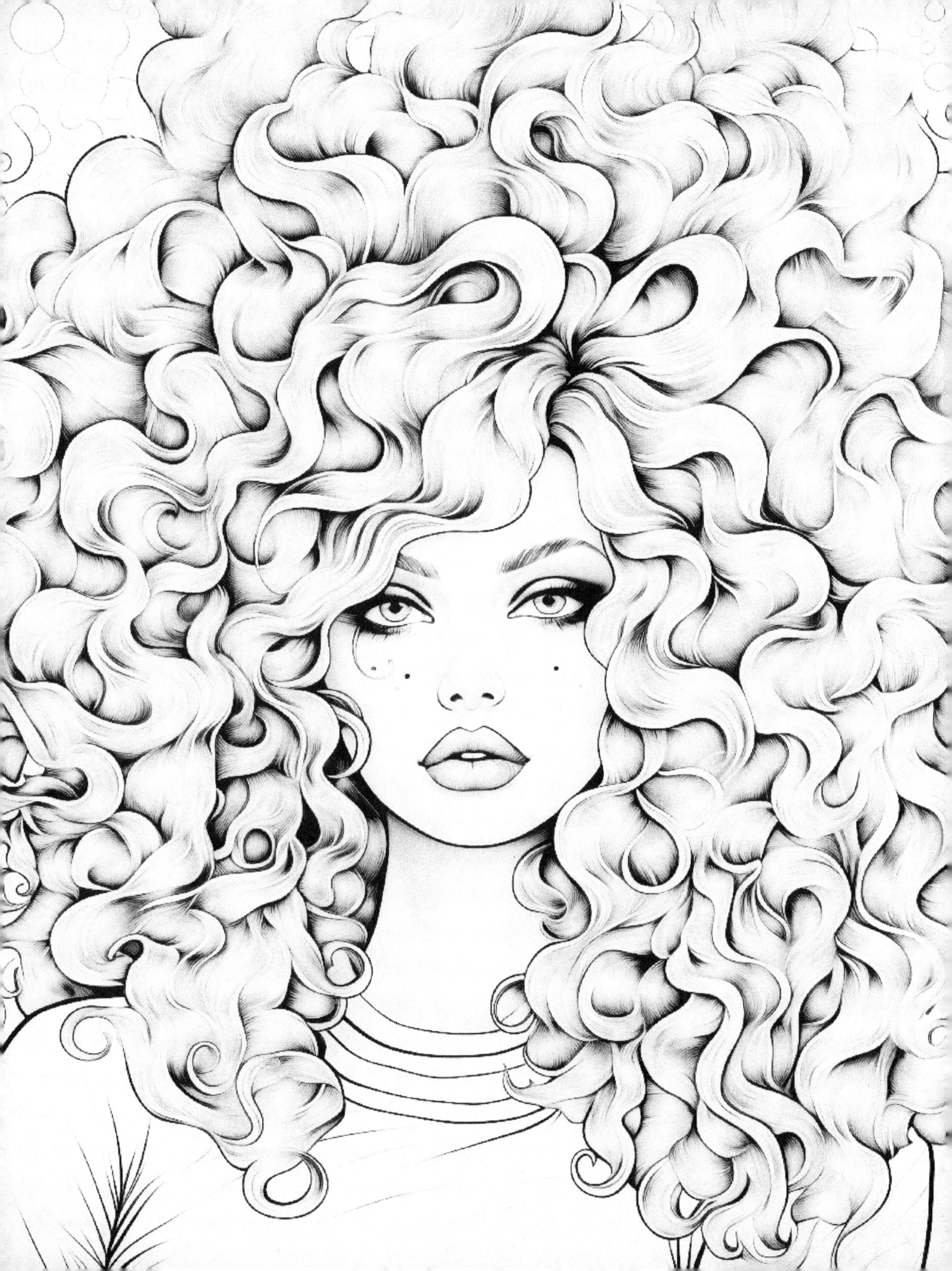

WASTE WATER TREATMENT

AND

WATER MANAGEMENT

WATER TREATMENT AND MANAGEMENT

DR. ANAMIKA SRIVASTAVA

Ph.D., M.Sc. (Environmental Science)
UGC-NET and ASRB-NET Qualified (EVS)

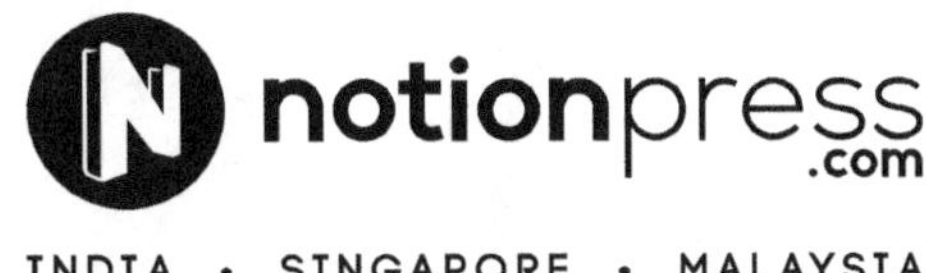

notionpress.com

INDIA · SINGAPORE · MALAYSIA

Notion Press

Old No. 38, New No. 6
McNichols Road, Chetpet
Chennai - 600 031

First Published by Notion Press 2018
Copyright © Anamika Srivastava 2018
All Rights Reserved.

ISBN 978-1-64249-783-0